VIS ON
MEETS
EXECUT ON

MASTERING THE CONCEPT THAT WILL DRIVE YOUR BUSINESS SUCCESS

DARRYL KENNA

 FriesenPress

One Printers Way
Altona, MB R0G 0B0
Canada

www.friesenpress.com

ISBN
978-1-03-914540-5 (Hardcover)
978-1-03-914539-9 (Paperback)
978-1-03-914541-2 (eBook)

1. BUSINESS & ECONOMICS, MANAGEMENT

Distributed to the trade by The Ingram Book Company

ACKNOWLEDGEMENTS

The writing of this book, and the process and time it required, was a labour of love for me. Through moments of reflection during this journey, I uncovered heartwarming insight and appreciation that I had not considered prior to this endeavour. The first was for the field of business and all the wonderful aspects that are contained under this expansive category. My lengthy journey within the business world has led me to countless relationships and opportunities that have helped shape my life in a positive way. Without business, I would not have found myself in life. I would not trade the education I have received through my experiences in the business world for anything. It is priceless in my eyes.

Secondly, I gained an immense appreciation for the writers of the world and what they sacrifice to share a piece of themselves and their lives within every book written. For all those who write books, thank you for adding to the library of life. As is often the case with many writers, this book has actually been in the works for years; now was simply the time to write it. While doing so, I often thought about this Nietzsche quotation: "A good writer possesses not only his own spirit but also the spirit of his friends." The people I have encountered in my life's journey unknowingly have been the foundation of this book, so it is important that I acknowledge them.

I want to thank the members of my test group, who read all the chapters I sent them and gave me feedback on the book prior to its completion. It helped to polish up a rough idea. Jeff, Nathan, Mike, Roy, Trish, Matt, Devon, Justin, Savannah, Terri Ann, Darcy, Amber, Peter, Corey, and Braden, your time was appreciated and means more to me than you know.

To my associates in business over the years and the businesses I still consult with today, please know that my exposure to your businesses and to yourselves helped to develop my skill, which provided the basis for this book. These relationships are very much appreciated, and I wish all of you continued success.

To my mentors, Gordie and Tom: Thanks for taking a chance on me. It has made all the difference and helped bring me to this place. I hope I have made you both proud. I wish you were both still here so we could celebrate this accomplishment together.

To my Epiphany Group team, who provides me the opportunity to live out my book every day through my role as CEO: I am forever in your debt. We journey together as team, and you are an important part of my life. Keep dreaming big.

To Angie (my Dawn), who has been in business with me for nearly twenty years: You have walked this journey beside me, and with your character, integrity, and grace, you are the epitome of what a COO should be. Thanks for your support, friendship, and inspiration over the years. You helped make this dream possible.

To the love of my life, Renae. Every day, you allow me to be the best me. You provide the inspiration I need to push the limits of who I

ACKNOWLEDGEMENTS

can be and what I can offer the world. I cherish the world we have together and all parts of it, including Precious and Puppino.

To my mom, who taught me the lasting lesson of not listening to the world and carving out my own path: I will never forget the question that you asked, with tears in your eyes, of a teenaged me: "When will you stop listening to others and do what you want to do?" The answer, Mom, was from that day forward. Thanks for the lesson.

A special thanks to my Uncle Bert, who inspired me and gave me perspective on the journey of life. I treasured my last trip to see you in Texas, during which I read to you the first block of chapters. Your phone calls to me afterwards, sharing your thoughts, were precious, and they inspired me to push forward. I will cherish these memories and hold them in my heart forever. I'm certain they have a library in heaven where you can read the completed version. Hope you like it. If not, you can give me a call to discuss.

INTRODUCTION

"It is good to have an end to journey toward;
but it is the journey that matters, in the end."
—Ernest Hemingway

Too often in business and in life, we feel the need to hurry and travel a long way from where we are in the search for a destination that will provide "the secret" or understanding we desire. Upon arriving at this elusive understanding, we think that all of our business worries and concerns will be solved. But alas, to our dismay, this destiny always seems to be just out of reach. Business owners need to understand that most businesses never arrive at the very place they set out for. By pursuing this business-destination approach, money often runs out, dreams are shattered, and families are devasted. By the time business owners discover that the true answers have always been right at their fingertips and within reach, it is too late. The knowledge we're seeking, that we so vehemently desire, is not found at the destination. It is present at all points along our journey.

I have spent the last twenty-five years—as a business owner, consultant, and mentor—immersed in a journey of understanding the true essence of business. What drives business in its simplest form? In this book, I want to share with you my knowledge and understanding of this very journey—a journey that has led me to understand that when it comes right down to it, business boils down to one key concept, a simple one that can be mastered and put into play in any business to change its path for the better.

Why is this simplistic approach needed for business?

The answer is rooted in sobering statistics, which show that most businesses will not survive in the first ten years. Regardless of industry and economic factors, these statistics continue to bear out the fact that there are other factors in play. This means businesses are not as strong as their owners think or pretend them to be and are actually closer to going out of business than they are to actually prospering. We need to change that.

Statistics don't lie, and the stark reality they offer paints a not-so-glamourous or prosperous vision of what owning our own business will actually be like. If we pulled the curtains back on business ownership, for many people at least, it is just a glorified job. And glorified or not, it's a job that takes lots of hard work and has a lot of risk attached to it. When you factor in the financial investment most owners tie up in their businesses, it puts many families in a precarious position. What compounds the risk even more is that some of the money invested in a business might not even be the owners' but rather that of their friends or families. In this case, the hazards of failure put even more people, more *relationships*, at risk. A great deal of that risk hinges on how a business is run.

What is this one key concept could help business owners?

VISION (CEO) MEETS EXECUTION (COO)

This one key concept, a two-pronged approach, is in effect in all successful companies. These two key foundational components—Vision and Execution, and their interaction with one another—are the key to the success of any business, regardless of size.

By using and understanding this simple concept and having someone officially fill each of these two roles (CEO and COO), we can transform any company with surprising results. The best news for you and your business is that this approach can be taught and honed over time.

Businesspeople who are open to learning and understanding this concept, and how it will positively impact their business, will benefit from this read and be able to apply the approach consistently until it becomes part of the very DNA of their business.

Like many of you, I often find the reading of business manuals and textbooks challenging, with the material typically presented in a very dry manner. As such, I have decided to share my insights and advice in a medium that might be a bit more pleasant and entertaining. Framed as a story, with fictional people and details but factual advice, I hope that the characters and situations I've come up with will be enjoyable along the way, even as it inspires you to make positive changes to your business model. Enjoy!

TABLE OF CONTENTS

CHAPTER ONE

THE FISHING TRIP

*W*hy on earth did I agree to this trip anyway? This was the puzzling question I kept asking myself. Of course, it really wasn't that hard to understand, given that I'd orchestrated all the steps that led up to the answer. I had asked my dad for his thoughts on a business situation I was dealing with and had inadvertently given him green light to give me his "advice" on my business. As part of this round of fatherly advice, he insisted on me taking this fishing trip to see his old friend, "the captain." Next thing I knew, I had committed one of my precious Saturdays to going to see this buddy of his. My wife had told me to just go, enjoy the day, and see what unfolds. *What have I gotten myself into?*

I was feeling both puzzled and a bit irritated as I drove my truck down the highway. I shouldn't have been irritated, given that the road was fine, it was a beautiful summer morning, and the view was getting more and more spectacular the longer I drove. I knew I should be enjoying the ride. This stretch of highway, just south of Pincher Creek, certainly had a better view of the Rocky Mountains than my home in Calgary. I kept asking myself what was really bugging me. It couldn't be that it was seven o'clock on a Saturday morning in the middle of August, and I'd given up my regular Saturday golf game for this fishing trip. I chuckled sarcastically. *No, never that. I should be back on the golf course, having breakfast with my buddies and getting ready for our usual weekend game.*

My mind drifted to my dad's buddy, whom I was meeting for this fishing trip. My dad had told me that everyone called him "the captain," rather his real name, which was Gordie, and I wondered why. *Captain? Come on, what's with that? It is not like I'm going out on the ocean with the man. Waterton National Park is in Alberta, and we're a land locked province. Captain ...*

I started to think about different captains, hoping he wouldn't be dressed like Captain Jack Sparrow or wearing an eye patch. My mind continued to drift, progressing to Captain Phillips and his machine-gun-toting Somali pirates. I had to snap out of the visual. *The things we do for our parents.* I chuckled as I shook my head, trying to just concentrate on driving, but it wasn't long before my mind drifted to my dad.

When my dad gave me his business advice, I always found it hard to listen that closely. He wasn't even in the game and his advice never seemed relevant. I could never connect it to any practical application in terms of solving whatever issue I had going on in my business. Still, I kept finding myself in those situations with him because I never want to let him down. I also never had the heart to tell him that his advice didn't seem to fit. I'd just let him ramble on and try to appear interested as he gave me his "wisdom."

Dad and I had remained close over the years, but lately as I started spending more time on my business, we seemed to have drifted apart. Maybe that was just part of a father and son's journey—the

2

passing of the proverbial torch. I loved Bert, my dad, but I always found myself wondering what he even knew about business. *He's worked as an employee at the same manufacturing plant for thirty years. I don't even think he's ever been around a business let alone gained any practical experience.* But despite my doubts about his business acumen, I still couldn't resist the temptation to periodically run ideas by the man.

Which had led me here: driving down a highway on an early Saturday morning. I knew he'd gone out of his way to arrange this fishing day in Waterton National Park with his old buddy, so I would make the best of it. All he'd said when he called to give me the details was that the captain would provide guidance on my business and that I would remember this trip forever.

———

When I arrived at the gates to Waterton Park, I was impressed by its view of the mountains. Most people who live in Alberta (or come to visit Alberta) go out of their way just to view the mountains, although usually in Banff or Jasper, and I could see why. The Rockies were undoubtedly majestic. I didn't really know much about this park, even though it was basically in the back yard of the area where I live. Breathing in the fresh air as I rolled down my window, I stopped to pay my park-entrance fee and then started the short drive into the townsite. At a high point on the road, the beauty of the park was on full display. I soaked in the colours and majesty of the mountains as I continued down the road. After a few minutes, the view opened up to showcase the Prince of Wales Hotel, nestled at the top of a hill right beside the two lakes: Upper Waterton and the Lower Waterton.

If nothing else, this view was worth the trip. I pulled over to take some pictures, then took a moment to read my directions again. I was to make my way to Pat's of Waterton to pick up my fishing license and then meet the captain at the marina. *This should be interesting.*

About five minutes later, I pulled into the parking lot of the marina, which turned out to be right beside Pat's of Waterton. I walked across the street to this quaint gas bar/store, which was the main hub of the park and fit perfectly into its surroundings. I quickly went into Pat's to grab my license, and once done, the young man behind the counter asked, "Do you need any information on fishing in the park?"

I told him that I was going out fishing with someone local, "the captain," and had to meet him at the marina. The young man smiled. "You're in good hands. The captain knows the lake well." I thought that was a nice endorsement of the man I was about to meet.

I left Pat's of Waterton and cut across the parking lot to continue my walk to the marina. Once I got there, I opened the private gate to the stairs that would take me down to the lower dock, and as I headed down them, I spotted what was surely the boat that was going to take me out fishing for the day: a twenty-two-foot aluminum fishing boat with two seats at the front behind a tall windscreen and another four seats in the back. Standing at the stern, a man I assumed to be the captain was waving at me to come on over. I breathed a sigh of relief. I'd been wondering about what the boat would look like, envisioning myself trying to cram my six-foot-three frame into some little rowboat. This one looked like it could actually handle the ocean, which made me relax a bit, as I wasn't so sure what it would feel like on the water today.

As I made my way down the dock, I could see the captain better. He wasn't as old as I'd thought he would be. For some reason, I'd assumed he'd be in his late sixties or seventies, but if I had to guess, I'd say he was in his early fifties, about ten years younger than my dad—though still about twenty years older than me, as I'd just celebrated my thirty-second birthday. As I got closer, I could see that the captain had salt-and-pepper hair on his head and a nice tan, probably from lots of time spent out on the water. There was a friendly confidence about him that made me smile as I got closer, walking along the dock, and once I reached the boat, the captain reached out his hand and introduced himself. "I'm Gordie, but everyone calls me Captain."

I was trying to concentrate on his words, but the name of the boat had just caught my eye: *In Search of Walter.* Beside it was a cartoon fish wearing an LA Lakers jersey that sported the number fifty-three. *What's that all about?*

I snapped back to the conversation. "Hi, Captain. I'm Mark. Bert's son."

"I know," he said, nodding with a grin. "Not that you would remember, but we have met before, a long time ago. Haven't seen you since you were around two years old."

I chuckled. "My memory's good, but not that good."

"I've known your dad for years."

After a momentary pause, while we both pondered what to say next, he shrugged and spread his arms wide. "Well, welcome aboard! It should be a great day on the water. No real wind to speak of. Hop on in and we can get ready to go. You got your fishing license from Pat's?"

"Yep. All set." Placing both hands on the hull to steady myself, I climbed on board and stood for a moment thinking I would need to find my balance, but this boat was really steady. A pleasant surprise.

"Great!" the captain said with a grin. "Let's set off."

As we pulled away from the dock, my mind lingered on the captain's words. If he had met me when I was two, he and my dad had obviously known each other even longer than I'd thought and were quite close, or at least they had been back then. I wondered why my dad had never really mentioned him before.

I settled myself down into one of the big leather chairs at the front of the boat as we quietly pulled out of the marina. Happily settled behind the wheel, the captain drove while sharing some facts about the lakes and surrounding area. Apparently, a devastating fire in 2017—widely known as the Kenow Wildfire—had burned its way right to the edge of town before a miracle had happened and the wind changed direction, saving the hamlet and its residents from disaster. As we drove along the lakeshore, traces of fire damage could still be seen, but as we moved farther south, the vegetation seemed healthy and normal again.

According to the captain's depth finder, and his own offered knowledge, at 458 feet, Upper Waterton Lake was the deepest lake in all the Rockies. I couldn't stop smiling just looking around, blown away by how beautiful everything was. I'd always known the park was here, but this was my first time seeing it in person. *What a hidden treasure!*

The captain had told me that we would be fishing in a place called the Goat Haunt on the far south end of the lake, over the boundary separating Canada from the US, and described what we were fishing for as "lake trout in the twenty-plus pound range." Although I was not much of a fisherman, I thought that sounded like a nice-sized fish and couldn't help but get excited at the idea.

There was all sorts of fishing equipment on board, and it reminded me of the boats I'd see on my beach vacations whenever I walked by the various marinas. As I would later find out, the boat had all this specialized gear not only so that he'd be equipped for guiding excursions on this lake but so he could take it out on the ocean and not be out of place. I could see he took his fishing very seriously. *Maybe "Captain" is fitting after all.*

As we powered our way down to the south end of the lake toward our fishing spot, the captain described all the bays and mountains that we passed. I found myself studying the man. I liked him, and he was obviously very knowledgeable about fishing and the area, but I couldn't see how he'd be able to give me any advice that would help my business. *Does he have some expertise or experience I don't know about, or is he like Dad, thinking he knows more than he does?* I suspected the latter was more likely. I resigned myself to the fact that this fishing trip was going to be a fun new experience but likely hold no actual business value.

Okay, I thought, *note to self: No more talking business with Dad ... or at least no more commitments to "business" trips with his old buddies.*

We arrived at the Goat Haunt at last, and the view was right out of some nature magazine. In terms of beauty, it was pristine and glorious and took my breath away.

The captain bolted out of his seat then. "Let's get set up." He got our rods set up, moving fast and deliberately, and gave me a tutorial on both the process of setting them up and what to do if I got a bite. I thought he was very graceful in the execution of this process. It was obvious he'd gone through the routine many times before. He explained that the boat would be trolling, chugging slowly along, and then it would be a waiting game. We would just have to wait until we passed a fish hungry enough to bite. "Consider it a test of patience."

Well, I thought, *time to relax and enjoy the day.* Little did I know that this day was going to be far from relaxing.

CHAPTER TWO
THE HOOK

I was studying the captain's face as he sat comfortably in his chair, soaking in our surroundings and looking like he was exactly where he was supposed to be. I was still trying to get a read on who this person really was and what he was thinking. I always tried not to judge books by their covers, but he definitely didn't fit the description of what I had pictured when my dad had suggested him as some sort of mentor. Who was this guy I was sacrificing my weekend for? Who was he really? If he *could* help me with my business, where did he get that expertise? I knew absolutely nothing about this man other than that he was an old friend of my dad, who apparently respected his business acumen

"So," the captain said, perhaps realizing that I'd be studying him, "I'm sure you're wondering what the heck you're doing on this boat and who the heck I am."

I grinned. "Not just a fisherman but a mind reader. I admit both those thoughts had crossed my mind. It feels like one minute I'm talking to my dad about business, and the next I'm sitting here in the middle of a lake, fishing with you." I shook my head. "Funny how fast things happen."

"Kind of surreal, I'm sure, but your dad mentioned that you've been facing some challenges with your business, and I promise I'm only here to help in any way I can. As we get to know each other, or know each other again, I guess," he grinned, stretching his hand outright at about knee-height (presumably in reference to how little I had been back when he first knew me), "I think you'll start to understand that my background and experiences actually do qualify me to shine some light for you in terms of how to tackle your business problems."

"Well, on that topic, I'd take any bit of light you have to offer."

"Okay," the captain said, leaning back in his chair and resting his clasped hands on his lap. "Do you mind if I start this conversation off with a few direct questions? They might seem very intrusive, or even rude, but I need to understand exactly where you're at with your business."

"Fire away," I said, shrugging and wondering how direct his questions could really be. I soon found out.

He nodded. "All right, Mark," he began, "through talking with your dad, I know you're *in* business, but how much do you really know *about* business?"

Talk about cutting to the chase. "That's quite the question." I thought for a moment. "Well, I'm no expert by any means, but I think I hold my own." I wondered if my dad had told him otherwise.

I had started my professional life in my early twenties, working part-time at the same plant where my dad worked, to help with the cost of my full-time schooling. After graduating the University of Calgary with a Bachelor of Commerce degree, I had switched to a full-time position with the plant, though I knew that working at the plant was not going to be where I stayed long-term. My goal was to find a career in which I could work for myself rather than being someone else's employee, especially at the local plant. As such, I had researched other business avenues.

On the weekends, when I wasn't working, I started to focus on financial-related interests, taking courses on mortgages, investments, and real estate. My goal was to see which one interested me the most and whether I could build a business on it. It wasn't long before I figured out that I wanted to be a financial planner, with investments seeming like a natural fit with my skills and mindset. With that decision made, I started pursuing a career in this field, passing all the entry requirements and getting my licenses.

I soon found a company that would sponsor me, rented an office on my own, and hung up my shingle. Business was slow at first, but after several months, I started to find my stride. As my business started to grow, though, it started getting a bit overwhelming, doing everything on my own with no support. On the advice of a friend, I hired myself an assistant to help with all the paperwork as I onboarded new clients. The hiring of an administrative-support person was a new experience, and I admit that I fumbled my way through it, but over the next several years, it smoothed out. My now two-person company had continued to grow, with me pulling in new clients, and my assistant helping with every aspect of retaining them. My personal life had grown as well during this time frame as I'd also gotten married. Everything in my world was coming together, but I was left unsatisfied. The business was doing well, but I'd still felt there was something missing in that part of my life. I knew there had to be a way to build a better team for collaboration and to handle more volume. I just wasn't sure what it was.

This last year, my third year of business, an opportunity to expand it had come along when two diverse financial advisors approached me about joining my company. The first was an older advisor. He was coming to the end of his career and was looking to retire and transition his clients. I hadn't been sure if it was a perfect fit in terms of my business, but he had a decent-sized clientele, and they would need somewhere to go. This retiring advisor proposed selling me his book of clients and staying with my business until his transition into retirement was complete. The second advisor had under a year of experience but was looking to work alongside myself for mentorship, wanting to learn more about the business. This move seemed to make more sense, as I could guide him while he added strength to the team, and it would give me some backup in the business for times I might need to be away from it.

At the time, I wasn't sure if I was ready to take on either of these opportunities, let alone both. My business was growing nicely, though, and at times it seemed that I could barely handle the work I already had. The more I thought about their proposals, the more I rationalized that I was ready, and I soon warmed up to the idea. These two deals would catapult my business, and I felt like I should be able to handle it. *How hard could it be?* With my new "conquer the world" attitude, I had agreed to take them both on.

My new larger team had been born, and I'd immediately found myself in over my head. My "conquer the world" attitude now felt like the weight of the world on my shoulders. Instead of me conquering it, the world was conquering me! I could barely keep up with all the demands the business was putting on me. I had my hands in every role in the company, and I was going home exhausted every night. Something needed to change. It was at this point that I'd decided to hire Dawn, a skilled office manager, to help with my struggles. I thought this would solve all the problems. With Dawn's addition to the existing team, I thought that everyone would become integrated and move the business forward in leaps and bounds. Boy, was I wrong. The hiring of Dawn just added to the problems rather than diminishing them. The business was now in even greater chaos, and my stress level was rising. What was supposed to have been a simple solution to a problem was turning into an even bigger one. The business has only barely moved forward since Dawn's arrival and might have even moved backwards. Something wasn't right, but I couldn't put my finger on what that was.

"Mark," the captain said, snapping my attention back to the present, "I know what I asked might seem like a ridiculous question. A 'Captain Obvious' sorts of thing. And at first blush, it does. If you're *in* business, most people would automatically assume that you *understand* business. But the answer is not that simple. In my experience over the years, I've found that being in business or owning a business has very little to do with having a true *understanding* of business. Years ago, when I first started in business myself, this was my biggest weakness. I really didn't understand everything involved in owning and running a business, which came at a devastating cost. I just about lost my business during that time. I even had to get some financial support on which to survive and try to prosper. But it was a lesson that I had to learn ... one of many. I had to educate myself, with the help of a mentor, in terms of how a business is *supposed* to function or operate to be successful. I needed to gain a true understanding of it. Does all that make sense to you, Mark? Do you follow where I'm going with this?"

I nodded. "I think so."

"Businesses are at the mercy of those who own them," the captain declared then, leaning forward in his seat as if to keep my attention. "There is no proficiency test or qualifications required to buy, own, or start up a business. Anyone can do it in a drop of a hat."

I frowned a bit, unsure. "But I needed to pass tests and licensing so that I was technically qualified to meet with clients."

"Yes, of course, and those steps ensure that you're a qualified technician in your area of expertise, whatever that is." The captain stood up and moved over to the nearest fishing rod, fiddling with it as he spoke. "An accountant in an accounting business needs to be able to *account.*" He glanced over at me and winked. "They need to know what they do for the individual clients. But it's in the actual business surrounding those technical skills, housing them, that I normally see deficiencies. This is a common misconception of people in business, thinking that the only thing they need to understand at the highest level to succeed is the product or service itself. They assume that just because they are qualified at what they do *within* a business, this competency automatically extends to the actual business itself, the organizational construct that wraps *around* that technical skill. Most people focus on understanding the product or service while leaving the actual *running* of the business a distant second in terms of their priorities. These two areas are mutually independent of each other, but you need expertise in both."

Settling back down in his seat, which creaked a bit at the movement, he shrugged. "You might have fished all your life and know every species and trick to catch them, but getting your fishing license does not mean you are qualified to run a fishing-expedition service." He reached into the cooler at his side and pulled out a couple of cold waters. "Does that make sense?"

He passed me one of the waters, and I leaned forward to gratefully accept. As the sun got higher in the sky, the day was warming up. "I think it does. I get what you mean. Just because I'm good at financial planning doesn't mean I'm necessarily good at running a financial-planning business."

The captain took a long swig of his water, sighing pleasantly at the refreshment before getting back to business. "The reason I brought it up is that if we're not on the same page with these basics, recognizing that the business itself is different than the technical skill of the service provided, we won't get anywhere."

"Right," I said. "We have to be on the same page."

"Yep. Most people don't distinguish between the two sides of a business, so constructive criticism and advice about one without the other doesn't sink in. Although I've just met you, this time at least, in terms of a business discussion, I'm going to just assume you're competent at the technical side of what you do. What I'd like to discuss with you is the *concept* of the business that wraps around that technical side, which is the area where most people struggle. Sound like a plan?"

"Absolutely." I raised my water bottle in a faux toast, and he grinned at me. We both took a sip.

"So," the captain said, "how would you rank your business skill *outside* of your technical skill, with one being very poor and ten being excellent."

I considered for a long minute, staring up at the sky and noticing a large bird of some sort riding the air currents. "If I have to put a number to it, I guess maybe around a five. I'd give my technical skill an eight, though, at least."

"Sounds about right. A five is very typical, even for someone who's been in business for many years, which you haven't. Right?"

"Nope. Coming up on my fourth year."

He laughed. "Just a minnow in the fish world." He sighed and stretched out his arms. "I too was a minnow once, and I remember all too well that feeling of watching the bigger fish, trying to understand what they knew about business that I didn't. This was especially true in the early years when my business was struggling. That knowledge always seemed to be out of reach."

"I hear you," I said, nodding.

"Well, during this fishing trip, let's see if I can share some of that elusive knowledge with you."

"That would be awesome. Thanks." Just as I was starting to feel a little more comfortable with how the rest of the trip would go, the captain threw a curveball, surprising me with another question even more direct and candid than the last.

"Are you sure that you're qualified to be in the role of leading your company?"

I could feel my Irish blood boiling, and for a second considered throwing him overboard. Luckily, I didn't know how to operate the boat, so that urge quickly disappeared.

Seeing my shocked expression, he smiled reassuringly and put up his hands. "Not ready for that question, I see. Just hear me out. Your dad told me that you were the owner of your business. That you were its leader."

"I'm qualified," I said bluntly. "I'm the one who owns the company. Who else would lead it? Who else would be the boss?"

"The boss?" He raised a quizzical eyebrow at me. "Who else indeed?"

The captain stared at me in silence for what seemed like eternity, slowly shaking his head all the while. Finally, he sighed, then said something that made my head spin: "I'm glad we have lots of time on the boat today. If what your dad described to me is accurate, I suspect we're going to need it."

I looked down as I gathered my thoughts, staring at the waterproof carpeting under my feet and noticing one of the snaps to attach it was missing. What exactly had my dad told him? My mind was racing back to the recent business conversation I'd shared with my dad. All that I remembered was describing my stress that the business wasn't as strong as I felt it should be or wasn't progressing fast enough. I had told him that things seemed to have gotten worse since the hiring of my office manager, Dawn. I was frustrated with the fact that she and I seemed to be on different pages in terms of how the company should grow and be run. I blamed Dawn, in a lot of ways at least, that the company had taken a step backwards instead of moving forward at the pace I thought it should.

I looked back up at the captain, who by this time was staring out onto the lake. When he began to talk again, it seemed like he was talking to the lake rather than directly to me.

"In this lake, the fish start out as minnows, but with time, they end up being a trophy fish that any angler would be proud to have caught and be associated with. Time does its magic in all areas of our lives, but only if we allow it to."

He turned to me then and smiled. At that moment, time seemed to stand still for me, but my mind started rehashing everything that had led me there. I couldn't believe the progression of it all. This was all my dad's idea, yet there I was, out on a lake with a virtual stranger, getting slapped in the face with questions and opinions that I hadn't even asked him for. I felt like I was getting hit with one wave after another. This minnow was drowning.

CHAPTER THREE
CAPTAIN CANDID

"I want you to think about any business," the captain told me then. "Any successful business. Regardless of size. In every case, there is one factor that is needed to be successful. Do you know what that is?"

I tried to gather my thoughts. "A good leader?"

"That's important, but it's only a part of it. What else?"

"Enough capital or a great product?"

"Helpful, for sure, but not the key factor common to them all."

"It's not coming to me," I confessed.

"Let me run a scenario by you," the captain said, turning briefly to check out the gauges in front of him behind the steering wheel. "Let's say that you and I went together to the main street of any city in North America. On that street, you could pick any business, in any industry, and we would go in. No financial statements would be provided, but once inside, we would only have fifteen minutes to decide whether or not to buy this business. On what would we base our decision?"

I thought for a minute. "Revenue."

He chuckled. "No financials statements provided."

"Oh, right." I rolled my eyes at myself and then looked out across the water. "Maybe on how long they have been in business or what their team is like."

"Well, you're getting warmer," he said, waggling his head from side to side. "It *does* have to do with part of their team."

After a long moment, I gave up. "I'm stumped."

"Most would be." He drank the last swallow from his water bottle and tossed it into a small pail that was wedged beside the front passenger seat. "Within every business, from the smallest one-person company to the largest multinational firm, two key roles exist and need to flourish. How we establish and embrace these roles, paired with how they interact with one another, determines both the success of the business and the lack of it. No exception."

"Regardless of the type of business?"

"Makes no difference," the captain confidently replied. "With each role comes a singular purpose they need to adhere to. Each singular purpose, when combined with the other singular purpose, helps guide the business down the right path for it, propelling it to its ultimate success."

"Okay, so what are these key roles?"

"The Chief Executive Officer (CEO), who is responsible for the *vision* of the business, and the Chief Operating Officer (COO), who is responsible for the *execution* of that vision." He shrugged. "Vision and execution. These two purposes *must* be present and functioning for a company to be successful. The relationship between these two roles is the key to any successful organization. The dynamic duo of success."

As he continued, he started fiddling with the rods again, pulling more line out, glancing at the fish finder, and then letting the weight drop further. "So, back to our hypothetical buying scenario. The decision of whether to buy or not would be based on the existence of, and relationship between, the CEO and COO. We'd want to meet both of them to see how clearly they understand their individual roles and how they interact with each other. This combination will tell you everything you need to know about a company. Together, this duo is the lifeline of the company."

"Okay," I said, nodding slowly and considering his words. "But why just those two?"

"Because that's where visions meets execution, the best metric of functionality in any company. When this duo is in sync, then the business runs like a well-oiled machine. However, when these two key people aren't on the same page, the business sputters along at nowhere near optimal functionality."

"I guess that makes sense, for a big company at least." Having finished my water, I strolled forward and tossed it into the pail, then leaned against the side of the boat, watching the waves on the lake.

"They would have enough people to fill those roles. But what if we were looking at a business with only two people? Or even just one. When I was starting out, it was just me, so how would that work?"

"Good question." He nodded, and seemingly satisfied with the rods, settled back in his leather chair, which creaked beneath him again. "Ideally, we would get the people or person to fill all the needed roles. But it's conceivable that, in some cases, one person would take on both and need to keep track of both aspects of the company himself, which isn't easy. Still, as you say, that was the case when you first started and worked alone. Both roles are still present, though. You need to envision you are filling each role and what it means to do so. We need to think about who is filling each role and how do they *view* their role on a day-to-day basis."

"Hmm …" I turned my back to the water and leaned my hips back against the hull, considering. "You know, even though I've grown the company a bit over this last year, adding a few people, I still *feel* like we're too small a company to adopt or specify either of those titles … those roles. And so we don't really."

"Maybe not the titles, but the roles are there." Tilting his head a bit and squinting into the sun, he explained. "Too often, we think such things are only for large corporations. But if instead of looking at the number of people in the company, we start looking at the roles people play, we'll realize that every company has a CEO and COO, regardless of whether or not they have an official title."

"You'll need to explain that one," I said, chuckling.

"No problem." He thought for a moment. "Let's start with vision, the role of CEO. Let me ask you something: Do you have some idea of where you want your company to go?"

"Sure. I want it to provide great service to the clients and be a great place to work. And to be profitable, of course."

A crooked smile creased his face. "Isn't that a vision, Mark?"

"I—" My mouth clamped shut as I suddenly realized that I didn't have an argument. "Well, yeah, I guess it is. But I'm not a *CEO* for God's sake!"

He seemed amused. "By 'CEO' I just mean the 'vision maker' of the business. We need to forget about the traditional definitions and be open to new ones, creating a new paradigm and using the term 'CEO'—in *your* business—to give line-of-sight clarity for everyone *in* your business, especially yourself." He huffed dismissively. "We're too reliant on titles like these and what we think they're supposed to mean. What I'm suggesting is that the vision-makers of a business use the term 'CEO' to allow them to start thinking differently, to change their mindset. It can be a subtle change, but it begins with that one person and will open up a world that will allow for their business's growth and success. Are you following me?"

"I think so." I returned to my seat at the boat's stern, stretching out my legs and crossing my ankles. "Regardless of my actual title, or what I *think* I am within my business, I should start thinking of myself as the CEO. Right?"

"Exactly, and by shifting our mindset in this way, you'll look at your business and see it from a different perspective. The same approach is needed for the person acting as COO, whether or not they currently hold the official title. Their purpose is to execute the vision of the CEO, putting into action or operationalizing that vision. They need to understand the vision, prioritize it, and execute it. So ... who is the COO of your business?"

"If you asked me an hour ago, I would have said that we're too small a company and don't have one. But if I'm following you correctly, then that would have to be Dawn, my office manager."

"Precisely!" He sounded oddly proud of me, which should have seemed patronizing but somehow didn't. "Again, it's not the traditional definitions of the role that matter; it's only their thought processes and agenda. If Dawn gives line-of-site clarity for the people in your business, overseeing daily operations, she is fulfilling the role of COO. The people who fill this role are called all sorts of things, from office manager to execution specialist, but just like with 'CEO,' what I'm suggesting is that we use the term 'COO' within our business instead, in order to allow those *within* the business to start thinking differently and adopt a new mindset. Trust me, this new approach helps the person in charge of execution be successful. And in your case, Mark, this person is Dawn, your COO."

"And just changing my mindset and looking at me and Dawn as 'CEO' and 'COO' will help the business and everyone in it to succeed? Really?" I knew I sounded skeptical, but I couldn't help it.

He nodded firmly, not giving an inch. "What it does is put you both in a better position in terms of the company's vision (your vision) and its execution." What would follow would be clarity, direction, well-established roles and responsibilities, and the both of you starting to think the way you need to. There is a lot more to it, but even just getting that established would be a great starting point of understanding for the both of you. It would also help those within the business to have a clearer grasp of the business's overall organization, causing less confusion."

"Interesting." We *had* been having problems at times with people understanding their individual roles and where they fit within the larger hierarchy, which had to be confusing. "Okay, I see what you're saying, and I guess it *would* be a step in the right direction."

"Yup, it lets the organization as a whole start to live in the mindset of those roles and see more clearly exactly where vision meets execution. That's what makes a business really a business. Not the number of people within it but the roles that are being performed. If you have a business with only one person in it, but that person is thinking and acting in a joint CEO/COO capacity, it won't be a business of one for long. The by-product is growth. If, on the other hand, you have a business of only one person, but they do not think this way, they will forever be a business of one. Unknowingly, they aren't really a business at all. Instead, the 'owner' has just bought themselves a job."

"Most people in my industry actually do work by themselves, so does that mean they're likely not really in business?"

"Although their business card might say they are in business, we need to dive deeper to understand what the true reason is for them to be in the business in the first place and what is their practical understanding of what business is about. At times business owners are there for themselves, and it is more status driven to tell the world they work for themselves or they are their own boss. These type of business owners tend to be more showroom than stock-room ... meaning they are about appearances, not what is behind the facade. These reasons tend to be punishing for the business in the long run, as they are about the person instead of the business and outcome of the business. We gain the moniker 'business owner' quite quickly when we order our business card; unfortunately, often long before we gain the understanding of why we should be in business in the first place, or how a business really runs outside our academic or theoretical view of business.

I groaned a bit, though I understood his point. "There go my business cards."

He laughed quietly. "We'll work on your practical business knowledge versus your theoretical business knowledge, and it'll come quick, so keep the cards for now. All businesses should really start to think of their businesses with this CEO/COO approach. It provides clarity to the business and starts to accelerate the execution of the things that need to be done."

The captain pulled another drink from the cooler, raising his eyebrows questioningly at me. I shook my head. "Now, one more point to clean up," he cautioned. "There's one distinct title I purposely left out of the list of titles most businesses choose to use for the leadership. Any ideas?"

I thought about it for a while. "Nope."

"You used it when I asked you if you should be the leader of your business."

I sighed. "Sorry, I'm drawing a blank."

"It's 'boss.' And I left it out because, in my opinion, it's one that never should be used, spoken, or even referenced in any business setting. It's a divisive term that goes against everything I believe in with respect to team dynamics. It's almost always used in a negative way that drives a wedge between people. People use it to exercise power … to control and suppress others. If a leader is about empowering others and creating the right culture, then there is no place for the word 'boss.' When I hear that word, it reminds me of a bad movie or Netflix series from the sixties. Outdated. Everyone, including the CEO, works for the business. They are all teammates filling different roles for the benefit of the company."

"You're quite adamant about this, aren't you?"

"Indeed, and where this gets interesting is when someone with a boss mentality owns the company." He frowned a bit, as though imagining or remembering something unpleasant. "Just because you own a company does not mean you are qualified to lead it. Unfortunately, businesses have no choice as to who owns them. They just get stuck with them. These owners think that, because they own the most shares of a business or the business itself, they must be gifted at leadership or are simply entitled to it. Being stuck with a leader who's got a boss mentality has damaged countless businesses."

The captain was right on the edge of his seat, his voice having grown more passionate as he expounded on the subject. His conviction was palpable.

"What's worse is that the people who unfortunately work for a company under this type of antiquated 'leadership' are restricted in terms of both the environment they have to deal with and the ultimate fate of the business. Most employees in these situations learn not to say much about the things they witness or ideas they may have that would help the business. They don't want to express their thoughts, and especially not their true feelings, about their boss, as this could jeopardize their ability to make a living."

I'd been nodding along with him in agreement for a while now. "Too bad the business itself doesn't have a voice to express what it thinks of its leader or owner."

"It does."

"What? I was only joking."

A strange look came over the face of the captain, and his eyes got very intense as he began to speak. "What I'm about to tell you will make no sense at first. You might even think I've been out at sea too long—"

"You mean out on the lake?"

He chuckled. Then the wind picked up, chilling the air a bit. *Weird timing.* The way the captain was looking and talking reminded me of an old seaman about to regale a haunting tale from his past on the high seas. *Call me Ishmael.*

CHAPTER FOUR

THE EYES OF THE BUSINESS

"Your business is a living, breathing entity that just needs you, the leader, to hear what it has to say. It fully knows where it needs to go and how to get there; it just needs you to help guide it to its destiny."

"A living entity? No offence, Captain," I said sheepishly, "but have you been drinking the salt water?"

He laughed then, breaking the tension. "The water in this lake is fresh, so drinking it won't make you nuts. If I'm off my rocker, then it comes from some other source. But I meant what I said. It's easy to mock what we don't understand, though."

"Well, I clearly do not understand."

"This abstract idea of business is the key to understanding the steps necessary to guide one to the right place," he explained. "You need to hear what your business is saying to you and follow its path."

I couldn't quite piece together what he was talking about and started searching my mind for clarity. I was just about to ask him a question when a bell started ringing loudly, which totally caught me off guard.

"Fish on!" the captain yelled.

I'd almost forgotten we were fishing at all, but the captain suddenly leapt up in a blur of activity. I had little time to even turn my head. By the time I did, he'd already grabbed the rod and set the hook.

"You're up," he said as he passed me the rod.

The fish on the line was stronger than I thought it would be. It kept stripping out line even as I tried to reel it back in. The captain was ready with a net in his hand, awaiting the arrival of our adversary. It took me about ten minutes to manoeuvre the fish to the boat, mainly because I had no clue what I was doing. When it was finally close enough, the captain swung the big net into the water and scooped up my first lake trout. According to the captain, it was around ten pounds, though it looked a lot bigger than that to me.

Once the fish was in the boat, the captain got it unhooked fast and then got me to hold it as he took pictures of me with it. It was surprisingly squirmy after the long fight, its long silvery body sliding around in my grasp as I tried to keep control of it. It was surprisingly exhilarating. The captain then asked me to release it over the side, and as I did, I couldn't stop grinning. After a momentary pause, it got its bearings, and I watched it swim away. I wiped my hands on my jeans, turning back toward the captain and eager to discuss what had just happened, but he had other ideas. As fast as it had started, the excitement was over, and the discussion continued.

Without missing a beat, he said, "Too often, we don't take the time to hear what our businesses need us to hear."

I felt my shoulders droop a bit, realizing that play time was over, but then settled back into my seat and motioned for him to continue, which he happily did.

"A business clearly knows where it wants to go. We, as part of the leadership of that business, tend to interfere with its destiny."

I was digesting what he was telling me, but my facial expression must have told a different story as he startled me with his next question.

"Are you okay?"

"Yep. I'm just wrapping my head around what you're telling me."

"Have you ever watched those old Indiana Jones movies?" he asked then. "You know, the ones with Harrison Ford? It seems he was always stuck in a cave with some giant ball rolling after him, ready to crush him."

I vaguely remembered seeing that one with my dad a long time ago. "Yeah," I said tentatively, not sure what he was getting at.

"I want you to think about the giant ball as your business," he said as he tried to make himself more comfortable in his captain's chair. I found myself a bit distracted once more by the creaky leather of the chair. Finally, he slouched down a bit and clasped his hands in his lap again. "Your business, like that ball, knows where it needs and wants to roll. Your job, as the CEO, is to *allow* that ball to travel down its path. Now, before you ask, no ... the ball is *not* trying to crush you, even though it might seem like it at times. It just wants to keep rolling. Your job is to clear the path for the ball to roll more easily, and faster, and without anything in the way that will stop its momentum. Do you get the visual?"

I thought about it. "I do. Yeah."

"I am glad it is clear to you because it's not clear to most CEOs. If all business CEOs understood this basic concept, they would be the last person in their organizations stopping the ball. And it would seem ludicrous to think that any CEO would be building any type of barrier to impede that ball from rolling properly."

"The ball in this case being a metaphor for a business moving forward properly?"

"Exactly! Got it in one!" He winked at me again. "I have owned lots of businesses over the years and had the luxury of working with the people responsible for the day-to-day running of things. I've also worked and consulted with many leaders and CEOs in various businesses all over North America. Would you believe that the opposite is true? That most company leaders spend their time not clearing barriers away but unbeknownst to them building barriers to restrict their own companies?"

This was one of the first time the captain had given me any insight into his own business life, in terms of what his experience or background might be. *Okay, so he's owned a business and consults with others across the country. I guess I should listen to him.* I chuckled a bit, realizing I already had been for quite a while. My dad obviously had known something I didn't about the man. I tried to refocus on what he'd been saying a moment earlier and come up with a response.

"So they impair their own companies?"

He nodded. "Yes. Not on purpose, mind you, but through their actions, behaviours, and thought processes. They inadvertently create barriers to their own success. Lots of times when I visit, I walk in and repeatedly find them hard at work building those barriers, with the proverbial hammer in their hands and extra nails in their mouths. Those barriers will ultimately limit their businesses, but even as they stand there in their overalls and hardhats—"

"Metaphorical ones, right?" I asked, interrupting him to ensure I wasn't losing the thread of his narrative.

"Yes, Mark," he said, smiling. "They stand there in their *metaphorical* overalls and hardhats, staring blankly at me, and don't for a second recognize what they are doing to their business."

"Wow," I offered. "That can't be good for the business."

"No, it is not good. If they continue this pattern, it ultimately slows the business's progress to a standstill."

"So being a CEO isn't enough," I replied. "You have to be the right type: one who moves the company forward instead of in the opposite direction."

"It's such a prevalent problem that I came up with a way to describe it." He raised his right hand. "On one side, we have the CEO, the person who drives the vision and is the architect of the business, or more accurately, the pace of the business." He raised his left hand, letting his right one fall. "On the other, we have the ABC, as in 'A Barrier-building CEO.' The ABC thinks they're a CEO, but their actions and mindset are really hurting the company ... and themselves, for that matter. Hence the 'ABC' moniker. The name fits its definition as well as the fact that, even though they knew see it on their own, recognizing the problem with exactly how they're fulfilling the role they *think* they have, that of CEO, *should* be as simple as A-B-C."

I grinned a bit. "Cute."

"Clever, actually. On the surface, it might be funny, but this a problem for far too many businesses, but a lot of people in that sort of leadership position get away with it. You know why?"

"Not sure."

"Because they're also the owners of the business." The captain smiled. "It wouldn't be normal for the owner of a business to give themselves the CEO job and then turn around and fire themselves. Of course, in a lot of cases, since they're really ABCs, their termination would help their own business."

"True."

"I know. Now, you might be wondering how it's possible that the leadership of these businesses don't see what they're doing." I nodded. "The answer lies in the mindset of the CEO and how they make their decisions for the business, or more specifically, through whose eyes, whose *perspective*, those decisions are being made. The ABC's eyes, or the eyes of the business, which belong to the CEO."

"Hold on a second. I think of myself and my business as one in the same. You are telling me that's not the way I should be thinking about it?"

"Well, yes and no. *If* the interests of the business and the interest of the CEO are aligned, then the CEO is seeing everything *through* the business's eyes." He cleared his throat, taking a sip of his drink. "In theory, if you could always get the CEO and the business on the same page, that would be the ideal. The business is very clear on where it wants to go and has the correct sense of direction, and the CEO would act as the eyes of the business and guide it properly. If you look inside any successful business, there is the CEO who hears and listens to what the business needs and then consistently guides it appropriately. The eyes of the business itself should ideally be represented by the CEO of the firm. When the business and the CEO are aligned, they are seeing the same path through the same eyes."

"And what if their interests aren't aligned?"

"That's when the problems arise." He sighed and slouched down a bit in his seat. "Especially if the CEO is an ABC in disguise, which will only widen the gap in terms of where the business wants to go and where it is being led. That sort of incongruent leadership can have a devastating impact on a business."

"If I understand you right, then there's an ideal way to run the company, and that is through a *CEO* approach that represents the direction a business naturally wants to go, rather than an *ABC* approach that is not aligned to the business's proper path. Do I have that right?"

"Yes. You're both correct and a quick study," the captain proudly stated, tossing his next empty soda can into the pail. "Those business cards of yours will be accurate very soon. As leaders, we need to have a clean slate in terms of agenda when it comes to guiding a business. A CEO will allow the business to point in the direction of the path it should take, and their job is to guide the business in that direction. An ABC will often bring their own agenda or baggage into the leadership of the business, and this restricts its progress down that path."

"What sort of agendas are you talking about?"

"Behavioural or motivational ones, generally, like stroking their own ego, seeking status, or maybe masking their own fear and limiting beliefs, even as they're ruled by them. There are too many to list, really. Such agendas are common traits of people with a boss mentality. These agenda items have no place in the leadership of a business and will make the interests of a business take a back seat to their own limiting behavioural mindset. Those that lead with their own misguided mindset put tremendous stress on the business and its employees and threaten the long-term success of the business."

"So why the disconnect? Surely the success of the business would only support whatever agenda they have. Why get in the way of it then?"

"Because of a leader's inability to *understand this concept,* as it applies to both their business and themself. That is the primary reason that barriers are built and exist. Without realizing it, they cannot separate their own agendas, their own behaviours, and actually see the business through the *eyes* of that business. They can only see through their own, with a perspective very different from the one the business truly needs its CEO to have. At times they seem to be on track, but then their alter ego shows up, the ABC, bringing their own agenda back to the forefront. This is very tough on the business as well as the team members."

The captain turned away a bit, looking out to the water and turning the steering wheel a bit to the left, apparently manoeuvring around something. "The two sets of eyes are in a constant tug of war within a business: the eyes of the CEO, in alignment with those of the business, and the eyes of the ABC. It is imperative that the CEO wins this contest for the company to succeed. And when you examine the decisions being made in a company and break them down, it becomes apparent who is winning the battle: the CEO, or the ABC. The business wins when the CEO makes the decisions and loses when the ABC makes the decisions."

I think the captain could see the wheels turning in my head as I tried to process everything he was saying and how it applied to my own situation.

"Lots to digest, isn't it?"

"That's for sure." I nodded.

"Maybe I can help with the clarity through a practical example. Let's say you're in the service industry. Whether you are a financial planner, a realtor, or a mortgage broker, you have a product that your clients need. For this example, I'll lump all these service industries together, as each has a product at the root of them. In any of these service-minded industries, you can start a business of one, a business in which you are both the CEO and the producer of the revenue for the business. If we surveyed any of these producers, they would all think they were in business for themselves and for the CEO, right?"

"I would think so," I replied. "I certainly did."

"I want you to think about the way these sorts of businesses' producers treat their earnings or commissions. The producer believes they should have access to every dollar they earn within the business to fund their lifestyle. Accurate?"

I sheepishly acknowledged it. "That's what I do, and I'd guess most other producers do as well."

"Exactly." The captain smiled. "If the business had a voice, which it does, what would it say about this practice? Does it seem logical that the employee of a business, which is what every producer is within their business, sets the rate of pay for themselves? How sustainable would that be for any business?"

"Not very."

"Through which set of eyes is this type of decision being made? The CEO's or the ABC's?"

"The wrong set," I reluctantly answered.

"It's clear the business is asking a simple question of the CEO in this instance: Is the amount of pay fair to both the company and the producer or employee? The answer to this question will help clarify who is making the decisions and through whose eyes. The choices of who is truly answering has only two possibilities: the CEO, who has a process in place to protect the long-term viability of the company by instituting a fair-compensation approach for employees, or the ABC, who lets the producer/employee determine their own pay, which puts the long-term viability of the firm at risk. So from this scenario, from whose eyes do you run your own business?" he challenged. "Who makes the decisions? Mark the CEO or Mark the ABC?"

"Mark the ABC!" I blurted. As I heard my own words, I had to sigh. Within my business, I was living two lives, both as a CEO and ABC. And I thought I could see another instance where I was dropping the CEO ball and carrying the ABC ball, though I wasn't ready to admit it yet.

The captain just smiled in acknowledgement and then continued. "Way too often when someone looks at their own business they get fooled into thinking there is only them in the business, so why wouldn't they just do what they want? This is a very short-sighted ABC approach, as it does not position them for the future. One should always set up their business for the future and run it as if they were in that future right now. Does that make sense, Mark?"

"Yeah," I confessed, "it does the way you explain it."

"Regardless of the number of people in a business at present, there always needs to be a business CEO making decisions that are in the best interest of the business in the long-term as well. We need to get in the habit of thinking we're a business with many employees, even if we're currently not, and conduct ourselves accordingly."

"Since we might end up there one day, we should start acting like it now."

"Exactly. We must start to think this way so we can see the business through its eyes as we act as the CEO of the company and guide the vision. We must guard against allowing the ABC to ever enter our business or gain strength within it."

The captain's attention momentarily went to one of the rods, as it was moving differently, but he quickly turned his head back toward me and spoke without missing a beat. "Sometimes we just can't see it as easily or understand it in those terms. Over time we need to train ourselves to think this way, though, to give the business its best opportunity to be all that it can be."

I nodded, smiling at him. "I get it now, and I'm fully on board." I patted my thighs. "And I've got the sea legs to prove it."

"Getting hungry? The best part of fishing trips are the snacks." He proceeded to open a container full of Hawkins Cheezies, pepperoni sticks, a vegetable assortment, and some fresh fruit. "Dig in!"

My mind started racing as I crunched on a celery stick. *Which one of the two Marks is eating celery right now?* I asked myself. *What am I thinking? Maybe I'm in over my head in this business thing ... for that matter, do I even have a business?*

CHAPTER FIVE

THE DYNAMIC DUO

As I was standing and stretching after checking all the rods, I took a deep breath and then removed my hat and ran my hand through my hair. The fresh air was great. I surveyed the landscape. There was one particularly beautiful mountain that stood out amongst all others. It had some real character to it, with a section that was quite ... spikey. It looked like the back of a dragon.

"What mountain is that?" I asked the captain.

"Citadel Peak, one of the most picturesque mountains in this range. I call it the Seven Sisters, though, for each of the spikes."

The points on the mountain seemed to give me some strength, so I jumped back into our discussion. "I was thinking about something you said earlier. You said something like ... if what my dad had said was accurate, I *would* need your help. What did he really say to you?"

"Not as much as you might think," the captain replied. "There was one thing he told me that caught my attention, though ... one particular statement that made me think that you might not have a handle on your business, or at least that you were missing some fundamental understanding, and without it, your business would never reach the heights that it needs to reach."

"You got all of that from one statement from my dad?"

"I did, yes. Your dad told me that you were thinking it had been a mistake to have hired your office manager, Dawn."

"Do you *know* my office manager, Dawn?"

"No, I've never met her. Don't have the first clue about her, as a matter of fact."

"Yet you can deduce that my business would be in trouble without her? Who are you, Sherlock Holmes?"

"No, I'm not a detective. And I am not sure *how* your business would do without her."

"Okay," I said. "You've lost me. If you wouldn't know one way or the other, then why the concern for my business?"

"It was the fact that your dad's statement described a common situation that I believe occurs in most businesses, its impact often underestimated by leadership," he explained. "In your business, you now know that, at least from my way of thinking, you are the CEO, and that for all intents and purposes, Dawn, the office manager, is the COO. Granted, you don't each carry those titles, or didn't prior to this fishing trip, but in terms of the clarity of your organization, it's the same concept."

"I *am* starting to see the two roles clearer."

"When your dad said that you weren't sure if you had hired the right person, and that the business wasn't moving forward, what conclusion *should* I have come to? It stood to reason that the dynamic duo, the CEO and COO, who are the one-two punch for your business, was likely missing a punch ... or maybe two. As I explained to you earlier, this duo is the lifeline of any business. As such, I concluded that your business needed a 'life' injection."

I raised an eyebrow at him but didn't say anything.

"Given that I do not know which part of the duo is the real problem, I had to guess, but there are only so many scenarios it could be. Scenario one could be that it is 100 percent you who is causing the dynamic duo to be less than dynamic. The second scenario is that the problem is 100 percent Dawn. And the third and last scenario is some combination of you both. I have been around enough of these situations to know that it's likely the third scenario. A combination. Throw in the fact that both of you are new to your collective roles, and I would be surprised if it weren't that last scenario."

"But it *could* be it is 100 percent her," I speculated, chuckling.

The captain just smiled again. "I was leaning more toward it being 100 percent you, Mark, but I've settled on the combination. Given this, I thought you might be thinking of throwing the baby out with the bath water, so to speak, and I didn't want you to make an uninformed decision regarding Dawn until you understood the roles and concepts better."

Although I couldn't feel myself making a face, my look must have been priceless because the captain started to laugh before jumping up. "I better check the lines again and make sure everything looks good." I sat quietly as he went about it.

Once he was done reeling in the lines and then letting them back out, he headed back to his captain's chair and continued. "So tell me about how you and Dawn function as a unit."

I thought about it for a minute before responding. "Well, at first I thought we were a good unit and would have given us a passing grade. It hasn't seemed as strong in the last several months, though, so our grade would have fallen."

I looked over to the captain, who seemed content to just sit back and take in what I was describing.

I continued. "We *have* had a lot going on in the last year, so maybe it's just that we're both tired with all the changes that have gone on. I'm kind of lost on what to do, though, or how to get us back on track. Maybe I need to get more involved in some of the things she's doing. Pitch in a bit and take the lead on some of our projects."

The captain stared at me as though he were searching for words but finally broke the silence with a kind of strange question: "Have you ever driven a wide highway like the 401 near Toronto, or the 405 in Los Angeles, or the Katy Freeway in Houston?"

My brow furrowed in confusion. "Yes. Me and some buddies drove to LA one summer. It was a great trip."

"The reason I asked is that I want you to think about these wide highways as your business. Now, as you would have experienced, there are lots of lanes on these highways. At first, if you are not used to them, it can seem quite intimidating, with all those cars and the high speeds. But once you get used to it, you see that the vehicles and highway function in harmony."

"That's for sure. It was quite eye-opening."

"Just like the highways, your business can seem intimidating, but over time, you realize it only feels that way because of the newness of the idea or concept. I want you to imagine that every role that is required and being executed in your business is one car on that highway. Each role, or car, needs a driver. Each of these drivers have instruction on how to drive their car, in terms of their speed, which lane to drive in, the general operations of the vehicle, and how it interacts with other cars. Can you visualize this?"

"Sure."

"Your job as the CEO is to drive the CEO car," he explained. "Your instructions are quite specific in terms of its operation and what lane it is required to drive in. To start with, your car will drive in the far-left lane, the fast lane of this imaginary six-lane highway. How fast you drive in this lane will set the pace of the business. The CEO car is the pacesetter, and the goal of the pacesetter is to move the traffic along in unison. Granted, the speed of each lane will be different, but they need to move in harmony. Does this make sense?"

I nodded. "I think so."

"Good." The captain leaned back in his chair, and I suspected this analogy might go on for a while. "If you, the CEO, are to be in lane six, the far-left fast lane, where do you think the COO, driving their own car within a business, needs to be lane-wise? Closer or farther from you?"

"Closer."

"Exactly. The COO, Dawn, needs to be in lane five. The wheels of her car should be slightly touching into lane six so that she can recognize the pace of the organization from how fast the CEO is driving. Once she's figured this out, she needs to be responsible for the pace of the traffic in the lanes to her right. Makes sense?"

"Absolutely." I nodded.

"So if the CEO is in lane six, and the COO is in lane five, where do you think all the other cars—the other business roles—should be?"

"They must be in all the other lanes."

"Exactly. All other roles would be to the right of the COO in lanes one through four." After a brief pause to find his words, the captain continued. "In a lot of businesses, the CEO will make the mistake of just pressing the gas and being completely oblivious to all the traffic on the highway. Specifically, they will be unaware of the pace of all traffic to their right, in all those other lanes, so they end up outpacing their own company. The cautionary note here is that you, as the CEO, need to be conscious of the pace you are setting within your business and ensure that the other cars, the overall support system of the business, is not being left behind."

"Makes sense."

"Let's keep expanding this idea, okay?"

"Sure."

"It is imperative that each car on the highway stays within their lane. To do this, they need to have a clear understanding of their own cars. What makes it run, how to steer, and so on. This helps with the overall goal of staying in the lane that their supposed to be in, so that the traffic moves smoothly and in unison. If this is executed—if all the drivers know what speed their cars are capable of going, as well as its limitations, and are perfectly clear on what lane their supposed to stay in, and how fast they are expected to go—there should be no disruptions to traffic or any accidents. If the CEO stays in their lane, and the COO stays in theirs, handling all other traffic effectively, everything should run smoothly. But unfortunately, this rarely happens in a business. We all know there are accidents on the highway that cause lots of damage. But in terms of this business analogy, what do you think causes those sorts of accidents?"

"Distracted drivers?"

The captain smiled. "Nowadays that's a concern for the real highways, for sure. But in my scenario, the single biggest cause of accidents is inexperienced drivers who tend to swerve out of their lane, causing others to swerve or brake unexpectantly within their own. Which car do you think most frequently swerves out of its lane?"

"No idea."

"The CEO car from the far-left lane. Hands down. The CEO decides he needs to try going into lane five with his COO and help them drive, help them do their job. That happens more often than any other sort of swerving. Why do you think a CEO would do that?"

"I'm not sure."

"Usually, it's because the CEO doesn't have confidence in the COO's driving ability, or else they just can't relinquish control over the business. They won't let go of the steering wheel. They feel it's safer to drive two cars at once ... or try to squeeze two cars into the width of a single lane, which is not how they were designed. They won't fit."

I could feel myself getting a little fidgety. By this point, it was clear to me that I was guilty of that sort of swerving but was uncomfortable with him recognizing that it applied to me, which he obviously had.

The captain continued. "In the most extreme cases, the CEO decides to drive *all* the cars on the highway and won't let *anyone* at the wheel of their own car. In fact, it's like the CEO suddenly swerving their Maserati from their own lane, through the COO's lane, and into all the lanes to the right of the COO. Then just as suddenly, they swerve back to their lane none the wiser of the pileups and broken harmony they have just caused. Unfortunately, CEOs rarely look in the rear-view mirror, otherwise they'd see the carnage they had created and left for the COO and the rest of the team to clean up." I was hanging my head a bit at this point.

"So, Mark," he said, "does your Maserati swerve to the right often, leaving its lane?"

Yep. He knows. I was sure my guilt was plain in my expression. The captain must have sensed how uncomfortable I was because he pressed onward to another question rather than waiting for an answer.

"Do you ever jump in and start doing what Dawn is supposed to be doing, or go to people on her team and instruct them on how they should be doing their tasks? Fulfilling their roles?"

"Guilty as charged."

"Why do you think you do this?"

Realizing that my arms were tightly (and defensively) crossed, I forced myself to take a breath and really think about my motivation before answering. "Well, in my mind ... I'm trying to be helpful. There are also times I figure it's easier to just do things myself." Shaking my head slowly, I let my arms drop to my side, then let my eyes wander to the mountains again. "You know, I didn't really realize it before. But with your driving analogy and your questions ... I have to admit that I have a hard time giving up the steering wheel. I never really thought of it that way before."

"You're not alone in that. It's very common. When a CEO *does* swerve, giving help when it's not needed, it's usually with the best of intentions, but that doesn't change the fact that the outcome doesn't help. It doesn't help the COO *or* the business. We have to allow each person to learn to operate within their own lanes so that they can all get better at driving. By not allowing Dawn the freedom to drive in her assigned lane, even if the road gets a bit bumpy, we rob her of the opportunity to improve. More importantly, we don't allow her to become a true asset of the business, the person who could free you up to focus on setting the pace of the company, which is your role."

I nodded. "Yeah, I see that now."

"When you think about giving up control to Dawn, what scares you?"

"I guess that she can't do it as well as I can, making mistakes that I wouldn't have made, and then I'll have to clean it up."

"This's normal and a common occurrence in a business, but over time, it can really impair the success of that business. We need to trust the people we hire for certain roles to actually fulfill them...and work with them to ensure that they have all the support they need to drive their cars themselves."

He let that sink in for a moment and then went on. "When a CEO doesn't trust or allow their COO to do their job, to fulfill their role, it limits the COO, and all too often I've seen them simply leave the company rather than be restricted, or else the CEO decides they are not working out. This pattern plays itself out often, leaving CEOs going through a disproportionate number of potential COOs just trying to find someone they can work with. They never can seem to find the right fit. When I discuss this with CEOs, they deny the problem, saying that they did give those people that role, which is true in a way. They've given them the title of the role but not the autonomy needed to fulfill it."

He sighed. "There's an old saying, Mark: Monkey see, monkey do. In this case, it applies to whatever COO the restricting CEO eventually settles on. They end up following the example of the CEO, repeating the same pattern, not wanting to give away any of whatever autonomy they've managed to get from the CEO. They don't stay in their lanes either and end up interfering with all the lanes on *their* right, not giving their own support team enough autonomy to fulfill *their* roles. The pattern repeats itself."

I nodded, seeing his point. "Hence the shared blame you mentioned earlier. But it really starts with the CEO. I can see how a CEO could go through a lot of potential Dawns if they didn't understand this ... and how that comment from my dad might have been a red flag for you."

"If people within a business continually leave their lane, none of them can ever find the pace of the business or maintain any sort of harmony. We need to allow all our drivers to learn to drive their cars, improving all the time, so that together they can help increase the pace of the business."

We sat quietly for a while with our faces tilted back into the sun. I let my eyes fall closed briefly, reflecting on everything he'd said. When I heard the plaintive cry of a loon off in the distance, I opened them and looked around. There was no sign of the bird, so I just sighed and looked at the captain.

"I have to admit ... there have been lots of times when my actions likely didn't give Dawn the autonomy of the role I gave her. I guess I've just been worried that she isn't going to complete whatever task needs to get done ... or that getting it done, and done right, won't matter as much to her, since she doesn't have the same investment in the business that I do."

"We can explore that point further if you're up to it." He shrugged. "I'm happy to help, but maybe you've had enough for one day."

I chuckled at that. "Well, we're already here, and the fish don't seem to be biting, so I'm game if you are."

"Oh, I'm always game." He grinned at me. "Usually, the challenge is getting me to shut up."

"Fair enough," I said with a smile, making a sweeping arm gesture. "You have the floor, sir."

"All right, so ... you worry about her making some mistake you'll have to fix and about her not having skin in the game like you do." He thought for a second and then tilted his head. "Can you give me a real-life example?"

"Sure. I've got a good one that I think explains my point. It happened last month. I needed a transfer form completed, but it got screwed up. I don't know if it was Dawn or someone else on the team, but the transfer never happened, and it cost me an account and a client."

"Okay. So how are you going to handle this transfer process going forward?"

"Given this mistake, I'm going to have to put in a process where I check each time a transfer is completed to make sure it's done and correct."

"Is the solution you described driven by Mark the CEO or Mark the ABC?"

I thought about his question, wanting to make sure I didn't jump into the big net he was casting. "Well, it's a company problem that Mark the CEO *needs* to solve or it will impact the business." I was firm on this point.

"On the surface, implementing this process of checking for

yourself would seem to make sense, and it would seem to solve the problem ... if it wasn't masking the *real* problem, which it is. That solution is the equivalent of you driving from lane six to lane two. How much money do you think this transfer mistake cost you in the loss of that client?"

"Off the top of my head, maybe four thousand dollars," I said, feeling a bit irritated by it all over again. "Money my company could use right now. That's why I need to jump in to ensure everything is looked after and doesn't happen again."

The captain nodded. "It's very important for businesses not to lose money through their poor processes. I totally agree. But let's run the actual math out loud—with the understanding that this is just an outline for conceptual purposes. I don't want you to get lost in the weeds in terms of missing variables like the time value of money and things like that, which would need to be calculated if we were trying to get this dead accurate. This is just to illustrate a point. There is the potential for another four-thousand-dollar mistake, which you want to avoid, so you've come up with what you think is a good plan to guard against that. But this plan, this new process, will take you away from your regular role for about ... What? An hour a week? Is this about right?"

"About that."

"What's your bill rate, Mark? Five hundred an hour? A thousand?"

I laughed quietly. "I don't think it's that high."

"Wait. I'm not talking about taking your revenue and dividing it by the hours you think you work. I'm talking about taking your revenue and dividing it by the hours in which you see clients *and* oversee the direction of the company. In other words, the time you are supposed to spend in your own lane. You probably haven't calculated that, but I would say a very conservative estimate would be between five hundred to a thousand per hour, and likely more. For the sake of keeping this simple, let's use the five-hundred-dollars an hour figure. All right?"

"I'm just running that math in my head."

"Not necessary, but okay. If you take one hour a week and multiply it by the weeks you're available to work, and assuming you have two weeks off every year, this would be fifty hours a year. Fifty hours, times five hundred dollars an hour, equals twenty-five thousand dollars per year. Translated, you will have implemented a process that costs the firm twenty-five thousand dollars a year to prevent a potential four-thousand-dollar loss."

I rubbed my face and sighed.

"Again," he said, "as we agreed earlier, it's important that a business does not lose money through poor processes. Does this decision to implement this process make economic sense to you, as the CEO of the business?"

"Well, no," I said, chuckling ruefully. "Clearly not."

"So would that decision be driven by the CEO or the ABC?"

"In retrospect, by the ABC."

"Look, obviously we don't want scenarios that cost the business money, but mistakes happen. We just need to look at what *caused* those mistakes to ensure they don't represent a bigger problem or pattern. Did the car crash because of inattention or negligence or because the system that taught the driver how to drive was somehow faulty? That's what *needs* to be discovered, and it will not be if you simply grab the steering wheel to do it yourself. Every process has a cost, and it's an even bigger mistake not to recognize that. Grabbing the wheel comes with a cost ... financially and at the expense of the culture and team you are building. We just normally don't bother to calculate it. That's why I did the math for you."

His voice softened a bit then. "Mark, you need to trust that Dawn has the best interest of the business at heart and allow her to drive in her own lane ... even if she occasionally makes a mistake. Economically, her mistake (assuming it was hers) pales in comparison to the one you would have made by implementing a system where you wasted an hour a week of your own time as CEO."

"You make a lot of sense."

"I know, right?" He laughed. "I don't know about you, but I'm getting hungry. Those snacks just didn't cut it. So let's see what's in the cooler for lunch." He grinned at me. "This fishing burns lots of calories."

"Sure," I answered, though deep down, I wasn't sure about anything anymore after the captain's lessons on business. But I *was* gaining confidence that my dad had given me good advice after all.

CHAPTER SIX

BRINGING THE SHIP HOME

M y lunch on the boat tasted especially good for some reason. I'm not sure it was really the quality of the food, as it was simple in nature, but it rivaled some of the best-tasting cuisine I'd experienced back at home in Calgary. I suspected it was either the fresh air or the excitement of everything I was learning that activated my taste buds. I started to wonder what else the afternoon would hold for me out there on the boat. The captain had certainly surprised me with his insight into business. I wondered how my dad had come to know him all these years, though. After letting this question percolate in my mind for a bit, I decided to just ask the captain about it. *What the hell?* I thought. *It's not like the man doesn't like to talk.*

Throwing caution to the wind, I blurted out, "How exactly did you come to know my dad?"

"He never told you?"

"He just said that he's known you for years. Did you guys work at the plant together?"

"No, I never worked at the plant," he said. "I knew your dad for years before he ever started working at there. Your mom too. Your dad and I were business partners at one time."

"Business partners? You and my dad?"

"Yep," he replied. "Your dad was just a young man back then. How old are you now, Mark?"

"Thirty-two."

He nodded. "So he was probably five years younger than you are now, and I was just about to turn twenty. We'd met previously when we worked a construction job together and hit it off. At that time, neither of us had really found consistent work or a career we had our hearts set on. About six months later, though, a friend told us about an opportunity to buy an existing business. It was a mobility company—you know, wheelchairs, scooters, and the like. The older gentleman who owned it wanted us to buy him out so he could retire. Back then, neither of us had much money, barely two nickels to rub together between us, so the five-thousand-dollar down payment we needed to come up with was a big deal. The total price to buy it was fifty thousand, with the seller financing the remaining forty-five thousand. We both worked to scrape together the money from any source we could find: from friends, family, you name it. We begged and borrowed to get the cash we needed, and in the end, we managed. We got the amount needed and took the plunge."

"Must have been exciting."

"It was, and terrifying too. It was one hell of a risk." He paused then, shaking his head and seeming to smile at his much younger self for his courage and ambition. "In any case, there were three existing employees that came along with the business we were buying. You know one of them. Can you guess who it was?"

"No clue whatsoever." I was puzzled he had even asked. How on earth could I guess something like that? It was before I was even born. "It was someone I know?"

"Yes, you do," he said with a mischievous gleam in his eyes. "Very well, I might add. It was your mom."

My jaw dropped, and it took me a second to respond. "Wow! Dad always said he met Mom at some job he had, but he didn't mention that he owned the company where she worked!"

He laughed. "Well, he did own it. We both did. He was a good business partner too and always put the company first."

"I ... I'm just blown away." I found myself starting to question everything I knew about my dad, and the value of his advice, but the captain didn't let me go too far down that rabbit hole, continuing with his story as though what he'd just told me hadn't changed everything.

"For several years, we worked hard at that business, but we were well outside of our knowledge and comfort levels." He sighed. "It was a lot of work with very little return. We were already at a crossroads as to what to do about it when two things happened that forever changed all of our paths. The first was that we met someone, a client at the time, who offered to mentor us in business in exchange for the cost of fixing his wheelchair. We were just considering his offer when the other event happened."

He looked at me, smiling strangely. "That one was inevitable and super exciting, actually. You see, prior to that offer, your dad had already married your mom, which was great news to all of us, and he planned to start a family. As it turns out, just as we were offered the mentorship, your thrilled parents realized that they were pregnant with what would turn out to be a baby boy ... the same baby boy who is sitting on my boat today."

Once again, all I could think of to say was "Wow."

"Amazing how things play out, isn't it? In any case, with his family about to get another mouth to feed, your dad made a tough decision and left our partnership to find steady employment to provide for your family. He asked me to buy him out so he could go and get a job at the plant ... and that's where he stayed." The captain shrugged. "Given where the business was at, and what seemed like no clear path to financial security in the future, I think he made the same decision most people would make. We agreed on a price that was fair to both parties at the time and parted ways."

He stopped talking for a moment then, chewing on his upper lip, seemingly reluctant to go on. After a long moment, he sighed, squared up his shoulders, and dove back in.

"Unbeknownst to any of us, the gentleman who had offered his mentorship and advice (much of which I've shared with you today, or at least have started to) really knew his stuff. By some miracle or stroke of luck, I was the recipient of the gift of his wisdom and managed to take it at face value, absorb it, and apply it. Within twelve months, the business started to take off and never changed direction. The principles he so graciously empowered me with were the foundation upon which I built and grew my business. And all of its growth, all of the success I have today, are directly attributable to his mentorship."

A companionable silence fell once more until something occurred to me. "So my dad could have been part of that journey had he just hung on a little longer."

The captain nodded. "He could have, but sometimes we hit a fork in the road and have to make a decision. Your dad decided on one path, one I believe most of us would have made in his shoes. My circumstances were dramatically different, though. I was young and single, so I took the road less travelled. As the poem goes, it has made all the difference in my life."

I didn't know what to say or how to respond. I'd definitely gained some new insight into my dad. Though I didn't know exactly how successful the captain was, I had some idea, and my heart broke a bit for my dad, knowing he had missed out on something that might have been a lot more satisfying than working at the plant all his life. I was so proud of him, though. He'd put his family and their stability first. I wonder why he'd never told me the whole story. I remembered that the captain had mentioned how good a businessman and partner my dad had been and I regretted having doubted his advice for so long. I thought about him, and taking in all this information, realized that my heart was full.

The captain gave me some mental space and time to just soak everything in, perhaps knowing that there was no better place than on the water for a man and his mind. Close to an hour passed before I spoke again.

"Thank you for sharing that story about my dad."

"I was happy to. Your dad's a great person, a man I respect a great deal and hold in the highest regard. When he reached out to me and asked if I'd spend some time with you, maybe give you some business advice, it was a no brainer. I told him I'd be honoured."

He shrugged. "My mentor made me promise I'd pay his mentorship forward. I can't tell you how many of these types of fishing trips I've had over the years. Too many to count. I have done these trips and will continue to do them to honour my mentor, passing on the wisdom he taught me that made all the difference to the outcome of my business, and my life as well. Although the separate paths that your dad and I took were set long ago, I'm grateful he gave me the chance to help you out along *your* path to new opportunities. I already thanked your dad, but I want to thank you as well. It means a lot."

I could feel how genuine he was and just nodded with a smile.

Over the next hour, we just chatted about life and philosophy. I came to learn that the captain had always stayed in regular contact with my dad, discussing business, among other things, several times a year. As he and I shot the breeze, the fishing took a back seat, and the time went by quickly. Although we'd only caught one fish, neither of us were bothered by it. The number of fish wasn't the goal, or the reward. The true payoff was just being out on the water ... and maybe learning a thing or two.

The captain stood up finally. "Well, Mark, should we put everything away and head back in? The fish don't seem to be biting today."

"Sure. It's been an enjoyable day, even though we didn't get lots of fish."

"Well, we have one last chance," he said. "While we're pulling in the hooks, we tend to get a disproportionate number of bites. Lake trout like the commotion, so we might still get lucky today. Come grab a rod."

As per his instruction, I jumped up, grabbed a rod, and following his lead, I jerked the rod until the line released from the weight that had taken it down to the depths we'd wanted to fish. Once done, the captain barked out the next order.

"Bring up the cannon ball, and once it's up, we can slowly reel in the lure." He jumped up onto the back seat to see the lines better. "Nice and slow."

I leaned forward, trying to see what he could see with his polarized glasses.

"Fish following yours, Mark," he said excitedly. "Keep going, nice and slow ... You got him!"

My rod tip bent then, and I could feel the fish. It felt a lot heavier than the last one. "Keep pressure on the line," the captain instructed as he reached for the net. "Guide him in headfirst, and I'll scoop him out."

I could finally see the fish, and it was a big one for sure. The captain scooped it up as soon as it was close enough to the boat.

"Got him!" the captain declared. "North of twenty pounds for sure. Quick question for you. Does this remind you of business in any way?"

"What?" I asked, distracted. "I don't know. Am I missing something?"

"Sometimes when I've had a slow day on the lake, the tendency is to assume that it's just what's meant to be," he said as he worked to unhook the fish and get it untangled from the net. "But the day, or business, for that matter, can turn around very quickly if we stay the course and trust the process. If I still have a hook in the water, I still have a chance to seize an opportunity if anything happens to change the view of the day. The path of a business is very much like this. It can change in an instant."

He finally managed to free the trout and held it out to me. "Great way to end the fishing day. Let's take a picture and get him back in the water to grow even bigger."

As I held up my catch, I couldn't help smiling broadly, even before the captain got the camera app ready on his phone to capture evidence of my big fish story and told me to say "cheese." Next, he put his arm around me and snapped a selfie, which he intended to share with my dad. Finally, we put the fish back in the water and fired up the boat for the drive back to the marina. As we were stowing everything away, I thought of one more thing I needed to get clarity on from the captain.

"Hey, when I first walked up to the boat today, I couldn't help but notice the name and logo on the boat—*In Search of Walter* with a cartoon fish wearing an LA Lakers jersey. What's that all about?"

He smiled. "It's a reference to the movie *On Golden Pond*. In the movie, Henry Fonda's character fishes on Golden Pond for a large, illusive trout that he's named Walter. The LA Lakers jersey represents the lake trout, and the number on the jersey is the weight of the fish that I one day hope to catch: fifty-three pounds. The provincial record here has stood for nearly a hundred years, and fifty-three pounds would beat it. So just like Henry Fonda, I'm in search of Walter, or a fish weighing at least that much." He shrugged. "It's just a fun reminder for me."

I grinned. "That would be a huge fish. Would you mount it?"

He shrugged again. "I *might* let him go just like in the movie, though I can't guarantee that. To me, everything is about the journey, never about the destination." He looked out at the lake, imagining his very own Walter. "I just hope that I get the chance to make that decision one day."

The ride back into the marina was satisfying. I felt like a load had lifted from me and felt more relaxed. I had a lot to think about in terms of my business, and Dawn specifically, and about my dad as well, but for now, I just let myself take it all in and enjoy myself.

———

After the boat was all docked and secure beneath its tarp, the captain and I prepared to say our goodbyes.

"Great day on the water," he said.

"For sure. I really enjoyed it. Thanks for taking me out." I reached out to shake his hand.

As the captain accepted it, he offered his final parting words: "It was my pleasure. Great fishing, and more importantly, great company. Travel safe, and if you see your mom and dad before I get a chance to talk to them, say hi for me. I'm sure your dad will keep me in the loop about how your business is faring, and if what we talked about today had any impact."

As I walked away from the marina and toward the parking lot and my truck, I started replaying the events of the day and everything he had taught me. It had all been an amazing experience and certainly not what I had expected when I'd started out on my road trip early that morning. I was glad that the drive home would give me time to processes everything and plan my next steps, which could very well determine the long-term outcome of my business.

CHAPTER SEVEN
THE LONG WAY HOME

As I headed out, I was still in awe of the beauty of this place and the chance I'd had to see it firsthand. Waterton was a quaint little village, and it had a great feel to it. At that moment, it felt like home—that feeling you get when all parts of your world come together and things just feel right.

I was glad that this park, this gem, was protected and would be just the same in a hundred years and still there for people to enjoy. It had been such a pleasant surprise. At the park's entrance, I took a left turn and started my drive back to Calgary. After everything that had happened, I would have three hours to gather my thoughts.

The first thing that came to mind was the concept the captain had described as "vision meets execution." I guess in my business I had the two people who could fit the roles of CEO and COO, as the captain had described them, but I was wondering if we were ready for it. Although we were already doing some of what was required within those two key roles, I knew that following his advice fully would mean a fundamental shift in the way we'd been thinking. Going forward, if I were to really act like the CEO of the business, and Dawn the COO, we had a long way to go to reach the level where we needed to be, and more importantly, where the business needed us to be.

Are either of us going to be capable of living these roles and sticking to our lanes? I started to think about whether or not I thought Dawn was up for this challenge, for really being the COO, and then stopped short. *Who am I kidding? The real question is whether I'm up for it! Am I capable of meeting this challenge?*

I knew I would have to overcome some of my "boss" habits and leadership tendencies that weren't actually helping my business, and wondered where I had picked them up in the first place. The captain's words had struck a chord within me on several occasions, and it hadn't felt good. It was like he'd been holding a giant mirror up to me with every anecdote and analogy, and I didn't like the reflection. There had been a few times when I'd been tempted to argue my point of view, but each time it felt like I'd be bringing a knife to a gun fight. The captain clearly knew his stuff. He obviously had lots of experience, since he seemed to know exactly what was going on with my business. It was almost scary how he could know so much when he hadn't even really met me before today. After today's fishing trip, it was evident that I had a lot to learn about being at the helm of a company, how to excel in that leadership position, and the way a company functions.

I wanted to become the leader I knew was hiding within me. I'd always felt I could be a good leader, and at the start of this day, I never would have believed that this fishing trip could be the catalyst for my transformation. If I could just embrace and understand the concepts about which the captain had challenged me, it would lay the foundation for the changes that both my business and I would need to position ourselves properly for the future. As I kept driving, I felt myself getting super excited about what this all could look like in my business.

———

By the time I arrived home that night, my mind was spinning, and I couldn't wait to tell my wife about my day. I took her through it all and then explained some ideas I had formulated on the drive home, flowing out of me one after another. She was quite surprised at how talkative I was, which was unusual for me, and that it all had been inspired by meeting the captain.

She knew I had been struggling with the direction of the business, and that the grind was slowly having an impact on my mood, so she was excited for me. I was excited too. I knew that the frustration of not being able to see how to jumpstart my business was bothering me and had been for a while. Searching for an answer and seeing no end to that in sight had been grinding me down, but everything had changed with this Saturday adventure. I couldn't wait to see how this was going to play out for my business.

I dropped my dad a quick text to tell him that the day had gone better than expected and that we would catch up during the week. I said that I would come to visit him to tell him the whole story and that the captain had asked me to say hi to him and Mom and send his regards. I also thanked him for arranging the fishing trip and told him how much I appreciated it. I knew that the next time I saw my dad, we would have a lot to catch up on.

CHAPTER EIGHT
MONDAY MORNING CONFESSION

If I said I got much sleep on either Saturday or Sunday night, it would be an outright lie. I was so jacked up about what all this could mean to my business that it was hard to stay relaxed enough to get a good night's sleep. Dawn and I have a scheduled meeting every Monday morning, and this time, I was going to bring her up to speed on the fishing trip. There was only one question tugging at the back of my mind: Would Dawn be on board with all of this and open to this journey? Monday morning could not come quickly enough.

———

I was up bright and early on Monday, full of anticipation and (truth be told) nervousness. I was still quite anxious about the upcoming day and specifically the morning meeting with Dawn. I was trying to figure out why I was so nervous. Was it because I was worried that Dawn might not totally understand what I was going to explain to her? That she might not agree? Or was it because I thought Dawn would say she didn't want to go on this journey with me? After a lot of soul searching, I figured out the real reason: I would have to come clean with Dawn about me actually being a bigger part of the problem than I had cared to admit. In my approach up to this point, I'd lacked true understanding of business, and that had been impairing my ability to develop a solution for my businesses concerns. This meeting was going to be a game-changer.

As my wife noted, I had more "pep in my step" that morning, as if I were "ready to take on the world's challenges." Given her comments, my eagerness was evidently on full display for the world to see. As I left the house, she wished me luck on the conversation I was soon going to have. I replied with my standard line: "Thanks, I'll need it."

At that very moment, what I was really thinking was that the amount of luck that would come my way was directly related to my willingness to act, and today was the day that I was going to put my ideas into action. Luck would be taking a back seat.

———

When I arrived at the office, I said my good mornings to the team. Luckily, the Monday morning meeting between Dawn and I kicked off the day, so I didn't have to wait long to get to what was on my mind. If it had been later in the morning, I knew I would have been left just stewing about what was coming up. Dawn joined me in our boardroom, and we both sat down in our usual places around the table. Dawn was just opening her computer to bring up the agenda of items we would be discussing when I decided to deviate from our normal routine.

Here goes nothing.

I hesitantly started to speak. "Dawn ... why don't you leave your computer closed for this morning's meeting? I'd like to hijack our regular meeting approach so I can share some ideas with you that I've been thinking about all weekend."

"Okaaay ..." she said, obviously puzzled. "Is everything good?"

"Better than good, actually," I confidently stated. "Nothing to worry about. I just want to share some ideas and paint you a picture of what I've been thinking about."

Dawn just nodded, but I could tell by the look on her face that she wasn't sure if everything really was okay.

"As you know," I began, leaning forward and crossing my arms on the table, "I reluctantly committed to going on a fishing trip that my dad arranged for this past weekend."

"Yes, how did that go?"

I chuckled. "Well, it wasn't what I expected, that's for sure."

"That bad?" she asked sympathetically.

"No, quite the opposite, actually." I smiled. "It seems that my assumptions were all wrong. First off, the captain did indeed know a lot about business, which was a pleasant surprise, given I didn't know what I was really getting myself into when I committed to the trip. He actually knew a lot more than I could have possibly guessed."

"Oh good!" Her relief for me seemed genuine. "So it wasn't the waste of time you thought it would be? Did he at least have an eye patch, though?"

"No eye patch or parrot, sadly. He was quite normal really, except for one thing."

"Peg leg?"

I laughed out loud at her quick, deadpan delivery, the nervousness I'd been carrying around finally starting to dissipate. "No. Nothing like that, but he was like ... an oracle of business. His grasp of business concepts, and the lessons and advice he shared with me, might be the best I've ever been exposed to. I didn't see that coming, for sure. Another piece of humble pie I had to eat was that I learned my dad might know more about business than I've ever given him credit for." I had vented to her more than once about what I thought of his seemingly baseless advice.

"Well, it sounds like you had quite the Saturday out on the lake!"

I nodded. "I did."

"Well, I can't wait to hear about it."

"There's lots to tell you, but I want to start out our discussion this morning with the reason I was on the fishing trip to begin with. I confess that was because of a business discussion I had with my dad in which your name came up."

"Oh yeah?" Dawn said, sounding a bit suspicious or worried.

"Yes," I said, feeling my nervousness return. "When I added you to the team, I had high hopes that we would be able to push the business forward together. As we both know, this hasn't happened. Of course, because I don't tend to look in the mirror at my own business competency, I felt you carried more of the burden of blame than I did. It's always easier to blame others than to blame yourself. That's what came across to my dad when we last talked, which is why he suggested the fishing trip with the captain."

"Okay," Dawn said, still seeming a bit unsure but clearly making herself hear me out before passing judgement or reacting. I admired her composure. When she nodded for me to continue, I took a deep breath and dove back in.

"Before this trip, I was at a loss as to how to deal with the fact that it just didn't seem like we were on the same page in terms of the direction this business should be going. I know I come across as confident in the business, or even cocky"—I noted a subtle change in her expression that seemed to confirm this assessment but carried on—"but there are lots of times, inwardly, when I'm definitely not confident at all. Far from it. Deep down, I was really struggling with how to solve this and couldn't figure out what was I was missing. But this weekend, I finally figured it out."

"And what was that?"

"What was missing, apparently, was a fishing trip," I said wryly, "or at least the captain of the boat. While we were out there on that lake, it was like he held a giant mirror up to me so I could see my business reflection, and I have to confess that I didn't like what I saw." I ran my fingers through my hair, still uncomfortable with the admission. "It was apparent that the problems this business has been facing have more of my fingerprints on them than yours."

I straightened my shoulders a bit, made myself look her in the eyes, and got down to business. "So before we go any further, I want to start our discussion by apologizing to you for my faulty thought processes in the past. They were not fair to you. Furthermore, as it turns out, they weren't fair to the business. I was not being trying to be malicious in blaming you. It just came from a place of ignorance—primarily mine—in terms of how a business truly runs ... how it should. I truly am sorry."

"I ... I really don't know what to say." Dawn's eyes were wide with surprise, her arched eyebrows raised. After shaking her head a bit, she finally said, "I guess ... apology accepted?"

I laughed again. "Is that a question?"

She grinned at me. "No. No, it's not. I accept your apology and thank you for offering." She shook her head again in amazement this time. "You must have had quite the trip."

"I did." I agreed. "A much needed one, where I felt the weight of the world lift off my shoulders. The weight of uncertainty and its negative impact, personally and in terms of the business. And now I'm going to replace it with clarity and positive energy in terms of where we need to go as a business. I'm confidant that, going forward, that will be a lighter burden to carry."

Dawn just leaned back in her chair, staring at me for a moment, before responding. "I had no idea all this day-to-day business stuff was having such a negative impact on you. You hide it well."

I grinned. "My wife might not agree. At times, I've been a real bear at home because of this struggle. Just miserable. But now it's time for me to get back to being a happy, friendly bear and staying that way. That's where I need your help."

I could see Dawn was trying to put all that together in her mind. I could also see she was unsure of what "I need your help" might practically mean to her. I really had no clue where she stood or what that would mean for the business going forward, but I was confident that once I laid it all out for her, I would get my answer ... one way or the other.

CHAPTER NINE
THE DAWN OF A NEW ERA

"Okay. So I've got to tell you about what I learned from the captain during the fishing trip. For today, I'm going to give you the highlights and how I feel they fit into our business. I really hope I can manage to capture the essence of our discussion and the concepts he shared with me. It was a lot to take in and understand.

"The first concept he took me through was the way we look at what we're doing within our business. He explained that there are two key roles in every successful business, with no exceptions. These are CEO, whose purpose is establishing the vision of the business, and COO, whose purpose is the execution of that purpose. The business itself is the *intersection* of these two roles, where vision meets execution. Although the reasoning will become clearer as I go on, moving forward in both this discussion and this business, my new role is Chief Executive Officer, or CEO, of this company."

"CEO?"

I couldn't tell if she was amused or offended at the apparent arrogance, but then she smirked at me.

"I know, I know." I smiled. "Just bear with me. I'll get to that right away, but I need to start thinking of myself as the CEO: the person responsible for the vision and direction of the company. Believe me when I tell you that this sounds strange to me too, just saying the words out loud. We're not a big company, so it seems like overkill, but there's a reason for it. More important than the title itself is that I start to take on the *mindset* of a CEO and make my decisions accordingly. Does that make sense?"

"I think so."

"Good. Okay, so equally important to the outcome of the company is the execution of the vision's mandate. This is where you come in. *Your* new role will be Chief Operation Officer. The COO."

"Ooh," she said, grinning, "I like that title. Does it come with a new parking spot?"

Smiling, I shook my head. "Sadly, you get the responsibility of the new title, but not the status. Hope you're okay with that. The point of this new approach is that we both focus on our new purposes, vision and execution, on behalf of the company. If we keep these purposes as our overriding focus every day, then the company will start to function better."

"But aren't they a little formal for our business? These executive titles?"

"When I first heard them, I thought the same thing. But the more I let the concept sink in and started to understand the purpose of the approach, the more sense it made. I realized that it's not about how other people perceive it. I won't be getting a vanity license that reads 'MARK-CEO.' It isn't about status at all. It's about clarity. It's about ensuring that we, as a business, understand that vision and execution are critical to our success."

"And execution is my purpose," she said, nodding. "I can get behind that."

"Good. As I understood it, what the captain said was that these roles and their individual purposes are designed specifically to give both of us clarity in terms of what we should be doing daily for the company. And what we shouldn't. Once we're clear on the concept, then we need the entire *team* to understand it, so they don't misinterpret what we are doing and are clear on what we are doing and why."

"Well, having clarity within the business certainly makes sense."

"The captain explained to me that the true test of a company and its functionality is the relationship between the CEO and COO, between Vision and Execution."

"Between you and me, in other words."

"Exactly. I think we'd both agree that we haven't been on the same page this last year?"

She nodded. "I think that's fair to say. I knew we weren't clicking but had no idea how to fix that."

"Neither did I. I had no idea what was needed or what direction to go, but ... if we follow what the captain outlined, then it starts with us recognizing and clarifying our roles, the purposes we need to keep at the forefront of our minds as we operate within this business, each within our own worlds. It also involves both of us ensuring that these worlds are both pulling the business to the same outcome. This clarity, if we can achieve it, will set the tone for the rest of the team to follow suit. They'll have clarity in their worlds as well."

"Sounds promising," she acknowledged. "I'm with you so far."

"I'm glad. The captain described us, the CEO and COO, as the 'Dynamic Duo' of the business. But *our* dynamic duo didn't seem to be particularly dynamic, and he wasn't shy about making that clear."

"Must have been hard to hear," she said sympathetically, "but hopefully worth it. So how do we make our duo more dynamic?"

"That's a good question," I said, "though unfortunately, I really didn't get the answer to that on the boat." I sighed. "We covered so much from a wider perspective that he didn't actually fill in all the details. I didn't ask either. It was already like drinking from a fire hose. I might need to follow up with him on some of those missing details, but for now, I'll think it's best to just start with his overview."

"Works for me!" she said, sounding excited.

"Awesome. Now I just have to figure out where to start."

She laughed, standing up and moving to the water cooler in the corner. "Take your time." As she poured herself a glass, she looked back at me. "Want some?"

"I'm good, thanks." I waved my travel mug of coffee at her. "I've been planning out this discussion since I got home Saturday, but I think my nerves about getting started have left me a bit scattered."

"No worries." She made her way back to the table, pulling out her rolling chair, settling into it, and rolling herself back into place. "So," she said, straightening her blouse a bit and smiling curiously, "did this oracle just tell you what you were doing wrong? Tell you stories about the good old days?"

I laughed quietly. "Not really. Though he did spend a lot of time on a cautionary tale for people like me in the role of CEO. He described how there should be only one person in that role, or one version of them anyway, but that sometimes there are two."

"What, like a split personality?"

"Kind of like that, yes." I frowned, searching for the right words. "He said that there are CEOs and then there are what he called ABCs—"

"ABCs?" she echoed, interrupting me.

"That stands for 'A Barrier-Building CEO,' with the barriers being anything that stops a business from moving forward. I doubt I can explain it as well as he did, but it has to do with either viewing all decisions through the eyes of the business or just through the eyes of the person running it. Mark, the CEO of the business, is always looking out for the business and its future and looks at problems and choices through those eyes when making decisions. Mark the ABC, on the other hand, places his own interests over those of the business. I could see bits of myself in both of those."

Dawn was frowning, obviously trying to just process this.

"Don't worry," I said. "When he first explained it, I had a hard time following as well, but the more I thought about it, the clearer it became. There are times when I do put my interests, or my family's interests, before the interests of the business. I put my fears and ego before it as well sometimes, which harms this business."

"But…" She was shaking her head now. "That doesn't sound wrong to me. Why *shouldn't* you put your interests first? You *own* the business. You're the boss."

"The boss …" I muttered under my breath, feeling my body sag as the word emerged from her mouth. The captain was right. I was using terminology that had a negative connotation and was not healthy for my business, or at least I apparently wasn't discouraging it. Worse yet, I assumed the team was starting to use it too. Before my trip, I would have thought nothing about Dawn's comment, but hearing it now, I felt something akin to shame.

"Believe it or not, though, it *is* wrong. I need to look at all business decisions through the eyes of the business if I am going fulfill my role as CEO properly. My eyes and the company's eyes must be one and the same. When they're not, then I'm allowing Mark the ABC to take over. There can only be one CEO in a company. There's no room for Mark the ABC to take a turn in that leadership role."

"Well," Dawn said with an innocent expression, "that should be as easy as A-B-C."

I rolled my eyes at her, remembering the captain's use of the same line. "Clever."

"Thank you."

"As for me being 'the boss,' everyone on our team has a role within this company, none more important than the others. I will not be using the word 'boss' going forward, and as a team, *none* of us should be using it. The captain helped me see that it's divisive and hierarchical and does not support our team approach. In hindsight, I don't even know where I picked up all that boss garbage, but it ends today. We're a unit, all of us in this business. We're a team, and you and I are the dynamic duo who need to guide this company with vision and execution going forward. How does that sound?"

"I can 100 percent get on board with that, and ..." An odd expression crossed her face as she let her voice trail off.

I frowned. "You okay?"

"What?" She glanced up at me and shook her head slightly. "Yeah, sorry. I just had a strange feeling come over me. You know ... I think we're going to do some amazing things going forward."

I gave her a big smile. "I do too."

"So," she said, leaning forward a bit, seeming eager to get to work, "what's next?"

"Well, the last big concept the captain explained to me is about how we look at the various roles within the company and how they all interact. He suggested that I think of a business like cars and lanes on a highway. Each of our roles within the company represents one of the cars, and each of us fulfilling the roles are the drivers. Are you following?"

"I think so," Dawn said hesitantly.

"This highway he described is a six-lane highway, on which my car is the CEO car, and I drive it in the far-left lane. The fast lane. I set the pace. Your COO car drives in the lane directly to the right of me. Lane five. All the rest of the people on the team drive their cars in one of the remaining lanes. The idea here is that we all need to stay in our lanes and learn to drive well in those lanes. Your car is nearest to me because you need to understand the vision and the pace I set for the company, and when you do, then you're responsible for all the other cars, each in their own lanes within the company, supporting them in their driving. Still with me?"

"Yep, but I do have a couple questions, if that's okay."

"Go ahead and ask. I'm still new at this myself, but fire away and let's see if I can answer them."

"Well, my first question is what happens if we veer into each other's lane? There are times when our roles in particular seem to overlap."

"If I understood the captain correctly, we need to really make a concentrated effort to stay in just our own single lanes. He grilled me pretty hard, wanting to know how often my car went across into your lane, as well as the others."

"And how did you answer?" I noticed that she'd raised an eyebrow, seemingly challenging me to hedge my statements.

"Guilty as charged," I admitted. "I told him that I tended to interfere with what you're doing, thinking I was actually helping. I do this with others on the team as well. I admitted to him, and maybe to myself a bit, that I'm a bit of a control freak."

"You?" Dawn asked sarcastically. "Never."

With a bark of laughter that I quickly stifled, I nodded. "I know, I know. I clutch the steering wheel tight and won't let go—"

"More like all the steering wheels."

My eyebrows raised at the jab, but I couldn't deny the truth of what she'd said. I was actually oddly pleased that she felt comfortable enough to speak her mind.

"Okay, uncalled for," I said, suppressing a smile, "but a fair hit. I promise, though, I'll be working on that going forward. I'll need your help in this area."

She nodded thoughtfully. "All right, well, this all makes sense so far, but who decides when it comes to keeping each of the other drivers in their lanes? What I mean is, what happens if I think a driver needs to be removed from the road, but you don't agree. How does that work?"

"Good question," I answered slowly, thinking about it. "We didn't get that far in our lessons on the boat. My gut reaction would be that I would decide, but I have a funny feeling that if we asked the captain, he'd say the opposite. Ultimately, my gut feelings are what got us to this problem state in the first place."

After thinking about it a bit more, I decided to run something by her. "Tell you what, why don't I see if I can lean on my dad a bit and see if he could get me another meeting with the captain. But this time we both could meet him. Would that work for you?"

"That would be great! A chance to meet the person who rocked your business world! I'd be all over that."

"Okay, well, if I can make it happen, I think we could both get some clarity on these concepts and how to properly apply them. I think it's in the best interest of the businesses to make sure we're on the same page going forward. We've got a great company to build together."

Dawn just stared at me for a long moment, seemingly at a loss for words. Finally, she spoke up. "This turned out to be quite a meeting this morning. I wasn't expecting any of this. When you first started talking, I actually thought I was getting let go, so this has been a pleasant turn of events."

"I'm glad. I think we owe it to ourselves and the business to get some support in terms of how to build it. Give ourselves a chance to prove that we're both up for the challenge."

We smiled at each other and nodded our heads.

"Okay," I said. "Let me go to work on my dad this week, trying to coordinate that meeting with the captain. I'll see what I can come up with."

———

After the meeting ended, I found that I was quite pleased with what had transpired between us. I felt very good about the first steps we'd taken. If I were successful in getting another meeting with the captain, I was sure it would make all the difference. He clearly knew this business stuff inside and out, whereas I was just a fish out of water. The captain could clarify this new approach and answer both of our questions, more of which would surely come up as we embarked on this new journey.

I thought about what a meeting with both the captain and Dawn would look like and was both excited and nervous once again. Excited for all that we would learn but a little nervous because the captain was so direct and candid. I just hoped that it would have the intended outcome of helping the company move forward. Hopefully it wouldn't scare Dawn away from the challenge. The one thing I knew for certain, though, was that if we managed to secure the meeting, Dawn was going to have her eyes opened up wide when the captain started to lay it all out for her.

CHAPTER TEN
THE LONG AND WINDING ROAD

I arranged a time to drop by my dad's place for a visit, and on Thursday, when my workday ended, I went straight from the office to my parents' house. It was only a twenty-minute drive from the office, so it gave me enough time to think about what was going to transpire. I picked Thursday evening because I knew my mom baked homemade treats on Thursday, and I would be happy to sample some of these while my dad and I chatted. This wasn't going to be a routine visit where we just caught up and shot the breeze. No, this visit had a very specific agenda. First, I wanted to see if Dad could call in another favour and arrange a meeting with the captain for Dawn and me. And second, I wanted to discuss the information the captain had given me about their business partnership and how he'd met my mom there all those years ago.

Sure enough, as soon as I walked in the door, I could smell the delicious aroma of Mom's freshly baked treats. "What did you whip up today, Mom?" I asked, heading down the hall toward the kitchen, where my parents were sitting at the table.

"Chocolate chip cookies," Mom replied. "Your favourite. Dad said you were coming by, so I thought I'd make something special."

"Yeah," Dad said, "your visits are always special. When you don't come around, your mom just makes me plain bran muffins." I could tell he was only pretending to complain.

"Well, thanks, Mom. I'll for sure take cookies over bran muffins."

"Do you want something to drink?" Dad asked. "Green tea or maybe a beer to go with your cookies?"

My mom just rolled her eyes at the thought of drinking beer with cookies.

"Green tea works for me."

My mom got up, gave me a hug, and instructed us to go out to the deck, where she would bring us our drinks and cookies in a few minutes.

I followed my dad outside. I noticed that he had the yard all set up nice, neatly kept and perfectly manicured. The deck was looking great too. We pulled out our patio chairs from where they were tucked neatly beneath the glass-topped table and sat down.

"You know, your mom loves it when you come for a visit." That was my dad's way of admitting that he loved it too. I smiled, knowingly. *He keeps a lot to himself. Maybe that's why he never told me about his history with the captain.*

"So how was the fishing trip with Gordie?" he asked right away. "With the captain, I mean. Tell me all the details."

I could see that he wanted me to be proud of him for the solid advice he'd given me about the value I'd find in the trip.

"I admit it. It was much better than I expected."

This was music to my dad's ears, and his smile widened. Over the next hour, I described the events of that day, and Dad could hardly hold in his excitement for me and the business. He genuinely wanted the best for me, personally and professionally. He was on the edge of his seat throughout the conversation, and a couple of times, I thought he might just spring up into the air. It was a good thing my mom had made a big batch of cookies to help fuel us for the replay of events. We devoured them as we spoke.

When I finally finished giving him the play-by-play, I started thinking more and more about my second agenda item. I had skipped over the part where the captain had explained their history, and I wasn't sure how would my dad take me asking about it. I was starting to get cold feet, but I wasn't sure why, as it shouldn't be a particularly touchy subject. The way the captain had described it, I hadn't gotten the impression that there'd been any animosity or resentment. I think maybe I was just wondering why my dad had never mentioned it. Finally, I decided to just throw it out there and see what happened.

"Dad ..." I said, hesitantly, "one of the other things the captain brought up was how long you two have known each other ... and that you used to be business partners. You never mentioned that when you were giving me the details about the trip."

"No, I guess I didn't."

"On purpose?"

He considered this for a moment, then shrugged. "I guess so, yeah. I don't really know why I didn't mention it to you. Probably a couple of reasons. The first that comes to mind is that I didn't want to muddy the waters in terms of why you were going on the trip and who you were going to see. I wanted the focus to just be on you and him ... not on me."

That made a certain amount of sense, and I told him so. My dad seemed like he wanted to say more, though, so after that, I just sat back and let the conversation unfold.

"I think the other reason was that I still struggle with what happened back then," he confessed. "I sometimes feel like the fifth Beatle."

"Huh?" I didn't follow the reference.

"You know ... the person who left the group right before it launched into fame and fortune? What if?" he shrugged. "*What if* I had just hung on a little longer in the business? Where would I be today? How would my life have unfolded? I was the one who left the band right before it took off ... and I have to admit that I often think about that. The captain has done quite well for himself because of his decision to take a different path than I did."

"I'm sorry, Dad."

"No, no. Don't be. It's not like I dwell on it, but I do sometimes wonder how my life would have turned out if I'd stayed partners with the captain."

"I can imagine, but you and Mom have a great life ... and you definitely produced a great child." I grinned at him. I was trying to lighten the mood while still acknowledging his feelings. "I understand, though, why you would think about the path not taken."

"To be perfectly honest, sometimes I feel a little embarrassed about the path I did choose to take." For such a private man, I knew this was a big confession for him. "The captain's a great friend, but I know that ... when we're together, that choice and where it led me sort of ... lingers there between us, unspoken. I think that on some level, he feels bad for what happened and wishes I could have gone with him on the journey ... and so do I, really, on some level at least. We still enjoy our visits, though, and I'd like to think that when we both look at each other's lives, there's actually a small degree of envy on *both* sides."

He pressed the tip of his index finger onto one of the few remaining cookie crumbs on the plate between us and brought it to his mouth. "That might just be something I tell myself, though ... to make myself feel better."

I just sat there, trying to hide my astonishment that he was being so open with his feelings. *What did Mom put in those cookies?* Still, I could feel what he was going through and almost see his pangs of regret. He really had made sacrifices for me that I had never fully appreciated until now.

Taking a sip of his tea, he continued. "I've spent a lot of years thinking about the choices we make in our lives, specifically what we're willing to trade for the illusion of security and certainty. There's no doubt that the path I took provided that, or at least what we tend to think of as that. It was the safe choice. A well-travelled path.

And it's not that I regret it fully. As I get older, though, I question if the safer path is really the one we should always take. You would have been just as loved regardless of which path I took. It's just that, at my age, I wonder if what I call the safe path is ultimately less rewarding in numerous ways than the path we label as the uncertain one. The monetary reward of each is evident, but did I miss out in terms of being ... I don't know ... spiritually fulfilled? You know what I mean?"

I nodded but didn't say anything, enjoying seeing this vulnerable, thoughtful side of him. I could see him searching inside himself for the right words.

"There's a thought, or maybe an image, that crosses my mind often," he finally said, looking around as if to check that we were alone. "I've never shared these thoughts with anyone, not even your mother, but over the last few years, I've been thinking more and more about a graveyard and all the tombstones of the people buried there."

Seeing my expression, he quickly went on to reassure me. "I know it sounds morbid, like I'm focussing on my mortality, but that's really not it. Just hear me out, okay?"

I nodded uncertainly.

"It's like a scene from a movie, but I'm in it. I see myself walking among the rows and rows of tombstones, wondering which of the deceased had lived their lives making decisions that they thought were the safer option and which of them took the less travelled path instead. And what I've come to realize is that we all end up in that same place. All of us, as evidenced by those tombstones. So given this, I have to ask myself why we shouldn't take the less travelled paths instead."

I sat there in amazement, staring at my father and recognizing a depth in him that I'd never noticed before.

He went on. "Let's face it, books and movies aren't written about people who take the safe path, because what would be the point?"

I didn't know what he wanted me to say. Did he want reassurance that his chosen path had value as well? Commiseration that it didn't? Before I could decide, he leaned forward and got to his larger point.

"Look, the real reason I sent you to the captain is so that he could guide you. Guide you on the path of what most would call uncertainty—a path that over the years I've grown to understand is more certain than it appears but still one that most people choose not to walk. I knew he could give you the best opportunity to walk a path that's both fulfilling and rewarding in so many ways. Although I missed *my* chance to walk that path, I've learned about it through my many discussions with the captain over the years. *That* is why I sent you to him. Although it's a less-travelled path, it's one that you need to at least explore. The other path, the one most people travel, just like me ... well, that one will always be there for you in one form or another. It isn't going anywhere."

He nodded at me then with a big smile on his face, and I knew he had finished his lesson. In what I felt had been a surprisingly profound way, the words he had just spoken made the fact that he wanted what was best for me clearer than it had ever been.

"Thanks, Dad," I said, pushing my chair back from the table. "For telling me all that and for insisting I meet the captain. It means a lot, and for what it's worth, I'm proud of you, and of the life you built for us." Smiling, I stood up and stepped toward him for a hug. He got up, slapping my back as he wrapped his arms around me.

"You're welcome, son." Stepping away, he nodded. "And thank *you* for taking the first step down your path."

I just nodded. I really didn't know where to go from there in our conversation, so I decided to lighten the mood. "So do you think the fifth Beatle has enough pull to get me another meeting with the captain?" He laughed. "Dawn and I could really use his guidance, so we were hoping to meet with him together, and get some momentum going, propelling the business in the right direction."

"Oh good!" he said, pride evident in his voice. "I don't think that'll be a problem. I'm sure I can track him down on his long and winding road."

He winked at me, and I rolled my eyes at the Beatles reference, but I was happy to hear that he could make the meeting happen.

CHAPTER ELEVEN
VISION & EXECUTION MEET CAPTAIN

I t did not take long for my dad to track the captain down. Calling me at home later that evening, he told me that the captain was actually going to be in our area the following week, on business, and would be free on the Wednesday afternoon if that would work for us. I texted Dawn to confirm that this would work for her, and it did. It seemed the stars were aligning. I let my dad know to pass on the message that we would be open to meeting the captain at our offices at one o'clock on Wednesday. I think my dad liked being the go-between, setting this for us. He was quite excited about the whole idea.

That weekend, history repeated itself (as it so often does), and I found myself having trouble sleeping, both nights, in nervous but excited anticipation of the upcoming meeting. On Monday and Tuesday, Dawn and I both had a hard time concentrating on our work, and we both confessed to just going through the motions of our daily work routines.

Finally, Wednesday arrived, and I was in my office when I heard the captain arrive at our reception area. I decided not to wait for our receptionist to buzz my office and just jumped up to go out and greet him.

"Captain!" I said. "Thanks for coming for a visit."

"Mark!" The captain smiled. "Look at you all fancied up! Very professional. Impressive."

I laughed, glad that I'd given into the impulse to put on my most professional suit that day. "My weekend fishing attire might raise some eyebrows at the office, so I thought I'd better get cleaned up. We have a special guest visiting us today, you know, so we needed to put on the dog."

I noticed that the captain was looking rather spiffy himself, wearing well-tailored grey dress slacks that were just a shade lighter than his silk tie, and a crisp, white shirt. A grey blazer was folded over his arm. He looked every bit the successful businessman. It kind of surprised me for a moment before I remembered that he was in town this week on business. *Maybe he had a meeting this morning somewhere else.*

"Special guest, eh? Now who could that be?" He grinned.

"Why don't we head to the boardroom? Dawn will join us there." I gestured toward the hall leading off to the boardroom and turned to lead the way. "There are drinks available in case you need something."

"Great." The captain looked around as he followed me down the hall, taking careful note of the artwork and plush carpeting. "Quite the nice place you have here."

"Thanks. We're very happy with it. It's getting a little tight in terms of space with the team we have now, but we make do. We all love it here."

We'd just entered the boardroom when Dawn appeared, following us in and greeting the captain with a big smile. She was dressed quite professionally as well, perhaps a bit more so than she normally was, and carrying a laptop case.

"You must be the captain. Hello!" She put her hand out. "Mark has not stopped talking about you and his fishing trip. I'm Dawn, the COO in training."

The captain smiled and accepted her hand, giving it a firm shake before releasing it, a friendly smile on his face. "Did he tell you he caught all the fish that day? He's quite the natural."

"I think we both know I was more like a fish out of water," I said with a dismissive tone. "On many levels, actually."

After politely rejecting Dawn's offer of refreshments, he took a seat at the table (laying his jacket carefully over the back of his chair), and we quickly followed suit.

"Captain," I said, "Dawn and I really appreciate you taking the time to meet us this afternoon. It's true that I haven't been able to stop talking and thinking about you and our fishing trip. She wasn't kidding about that. I was blown away by two things that day. The first was Waterton National Park itself, of course, which by the way is just an incredible slice of the world. A beautiful, hidden gem of a park and a real eye-opener. I'm letting anyone who'll listen know what they're missing out on if they haven't gone to see it for themselves."

"It's true," Dawn added, grinning. "I think Marian at reception's his first convert. She's planning a camping trip out there for her next vacation."

"Me too, I think," I offered. "Thanks again for hosting me that day."

"My pleasure. I'm glad you enjoyed it."

"Of course, as you've likely guessed, it was our conversations about business that really took the day to a whole other level," I said, eagerness apparent in my voice. "I must admit that I was over-the-top excited on the drive home from Waterton that day. My mind was racing that whole weekend, as a matter of fact. Our conversation really got me going, making me feel alive and hopeful for where we could take this company."

The captain's smile broadened at that. "Well, I'm thrilled you came away from it so excited."

"Excited is an understatement," I confessed. "The first chance I got, I sat down with Dawn and brought her up to speed on some of the concepts you took me through. I'm not sure I did every one of them justice, in terms of how you explained them to me, but I think I got most of it right. By Dawn's initial reaction, I knew I was at least in the ballpark, since she seemed to get excited about it as well."

Dawn nodded. "Oh, I am. It all sounds incredibly promising."

"Excellent. Business *should* be exciting," the captain said, interlacing his fingers and resting his forearms on the oak tabletop.

"What I was hoping we could do here this afternoon," I said, "is expand on some of the concepts you started taking me through on the boat. I figured that rather than me butchering them, we should get it right from the proverbial horse's mouth."

"Well, that's why I'm here," he said. "I'm happy to offer you any help I can with your business."

"Great," I quickly replied. "Dawn and I are going to be sponges and soak up everything you're willing to share. So," I placed the palm of my hands flat on the table and took a deep breath, "just to bring you up to speed on where we're at, I've already shared with Dawn the concept of 'vision meets execution' and a brief overview of the roles of the CEO and COO. The dynamic duo as it were. I also shared your highway analogy and staying in our own lanes. It really was just an overview, though ... like from thirty-thousand feet up ... and likely has nowhere as much detail or clarity as what I assume you have to offer. So I guess now it's just a matter of where and how you want to get started."

He nodded, and then leaning back slightly in his chair and loosening his tie a bit, he got down to business. "All right, so ... as you said, you've already at least touched on a lot of what we discussed on the boat. I'll be able to sense what needs expanding upon as we proceed, but for now, why don't we kick off this afternoon's session by looking at the business from a clarity point of view. The organizational structure of a business tells us a lot about the functionality of the business. Do you currently have an organizational chart for this business?"

Dawn and I looked at each other and winced at bit. "You mean one that's actually on paper and not just in our heads?"

He smiled at us and continued without missing a beat. "Okay, so let's imagine that your business *had* an organizational chart, which I know will become an on-paper reality after today's meeting." He grinned. "This chart shows the roles within the organization, its hierarchy in terms of who reports to who, along with a picture of the individual that currently fills each role. This sort of chart, even in a one-person company, is still comprised of four to six roles. For larger organizations, there could be anywhere from fifty to a hundred roles. Every business should create this type of document, clearly illustrating what that compony truly requires for proper execution of its business. Make sense?"

"Yes," Dawn replied, beating me to the punch. I just nodded.

"It's important to lay out the roles that you think the company should have for the next several years," the captain continued, "not just the roles it currently has. I want to be very clear on this. If, for instance, you have ten roles within a business but only five people as part of the team, it should be obvious that people's faces would have to appear more than once on this chart. This would be especially true for companies with less than twenty people."

The captain stood up then and asked if he could draw on the room's whiteboards, set up on two of the boardroom's four walls. With our encouragement, he grabbed a dry-erase marker from the ledge beneath one of the boards and proceeded to draw a makeshift organizational chart, continuing to add details as he went along.

"For a one-person company," the captain explained, "that lone person's picture might appear in all six places of their organizational chart. At first blush, this might seem silly. I mean, why bother to have an organizational chart if the same person's face is all over it, right? But there is a method to the madness. Do any reasons jump out to you as to why we should really set up this type of chart for every business, even if there's only one face to include? Mark?"

"I would guess so that you can see which people you would need to have in the company long term."

"We have a winner! Give this man a prize!" He grinned. "Yes, indeed. One reason is definitely for the longer-term view of both where the company might go and should go. Care to double down on your bet and a guess another reason?"

I thought about it for a moment. "Maybe I better quit while I'm ahead."

The captain chuckled at that. "It also helps ensure clarity within the team whenever your business adds a new member, so that each member's role is understood. It provides a dynamic visual going forward as the two of you shape the organization. A visual that is an important tool in helping to bring everyone along with you as changes are made within the business. The changes could be adding people, as I just described, or it could be placing the people you currently have into new or different roles. With or without changes, it should be a document that all team members have access to and can see on a regular basis, and even more importantly, more than just seeing it, they need to have it explained to them so that the context of the visual makes sense."

I was so enthralled with what the captain was saying that it caught me off guard when I looked over at Dawn and saw that she was typing notes into her laptop. I had decided to trust that she would capture everything we would need to reference back to when we debriefed later, and I couldn't help but feel a twinge of pride, knowing that this trust represented a big step for me on my journey of releasing control.

"Our goal with the organizational chart," the captain said, regaining my attention, "is to clean up the business. This is where the *vacuum* comes in."

Dawn and I both stopped in our tracks and looked at each other, both of us clueless as to what he was talking about.

"I know what you're thinking," the captain said, smiling. "Yes, you heard me correctly. I said 'vacuum.' We need to vacuum the business through the organizational chart."

"We need to ... vacuum it ..." I was completely lost now.

"Yes, I want you both to visualize this action as something within the scope of the executive, which in this case is you, Mark the CEO, and you, Dawn the COO. We're comfortable with the understanding and use of these titles, right?"

We both said "yes" in unison and then followed it up with a simultaneous "Jinx!"

The captain giggled (which was quite an amusing sound coming from a grown man in professional attire) and nodded. "The dynamic duo in action. All right, so the role of 'the executive,' the two of you, is providing a *clean* organization by ensuring that all roles and responsibilities are fully defined, understood, and clear. If we view these roles as rooms within the house of the business, then we must be sure to vacuum each room (or role in this case) to ensure that it is clean and clear. Just like with rooms in a house, you start in the far corner and vacuum your way back to the door. Through clarity of role and responsibility, we leave someone to oversee this clean room within the organization. As we build out a business's organizational chart, each face will be replaced over time with someone else who will fulfill that role on the chart. If we continue to do this, over time we are left with a clear, clean organization. You should be familiar with this concept and vacuuming approach, Mark."

"I should?"

"Yes. Whether you recognized this or not, you did this when you added the first person to the team. Then you continued as you added everyone else. I cannot speak to whether you did a good enough job of vacuuming, of course. That's a whole other matter. But each time you added someone to your business, this is (in fact) what you were doing. Maybe not consciously or by a designed system, but by default, vacuuming was taking place."

"I guess I did, now that you mention it, though I suspect I missed some dust bunnies here and there."

"Quite possibly," the captain said, laughing. "That's where your COO comes in. Dawn, as you take on the COO role, you will be responsible for this process as you add and shape the organization so that it can meet the expectations of the vision Mark is laying out. To ensure that the organization functions properly, it's imperative that you ensure each person truly understands their role and responsibilities within it. How would you say the business is doing in this aspect as of today?"

"I don't think it would pass a cleanliness test," she said frankly. "If I understand your analogy, we've got a lot of work to do to get the sort of clean you're describing. Most of the time, we're just scrambling, unsure of who is supposed to do what and so on, and have not taken a process-driven approach to this. We're putting out fires, a very reactionary approach, instead of approaching it proactively, avoiding the fires by having everything spelled out clearly to everyone upfront."

I looked at Dawn and could see that she was feeling what I felt when I'd first started talking with the captain. On the one hand, the man had a real ease about him and explained the concepts in a way that made them digestible, and I actually found awe inspiring at times. But on the other hand, he knew how to cut you off in the ring much like a boxer would to get you in the corner and start punching you if need be. His jabs were quick and targeted, and it quickly became clear what path you were supposed to take. As he pummeled you in the corner, he was also testing you to see how you *handled* being in the corner and what type of "fight" you had inside you for the business. I could see that fight in Dawn's response when the captain got her cornered. For me, it was a great sign, and it was then that I knew we could make a truly dynamic duo and fight our way to a successful business.

CHAPTER TWELVE
WHICH HAT AM I WEARING?

"Ideally, in every company, we would have every role and responsibility laid out to perfectly match the organizational chart," the captain continued. "Furthermore, there would be a different person for each role the business requires. Unfortunately, that's generally not what happens in the real world. Most businesses cannot afford this ideal layout or are still in the process of working their way toward it, so for now at least, they must improvise. In lots of businesses, there aren't enough people to fill each role required, so there's some doubling-up, or even tripling-up at times. This holds especially true for companies that are just starting out. This overlap, with one person fulfilling multiple roles, leads to some problems that all businesses face. As I go on with this, I'll refer to it as the 'Which Hat Syndrome.'"

I knew that the captain always challenged his listener when he introduced a new concept, to figure out where they were at, and I steadied myself for the barrage of candidness I was certain we were about to face.

Pacing around a bit in front of the whiteboard, the captain continued. "The ability to recognize which hat is being worn in an organization—not solely which one *you* are wearing but everyone else is wearing as well—is the key to gaining the clarity every organization needs to run effectively." He looked at each of us in turn. "Have I lost you or are we still good?"

"Good," I confirmed.

"We're with you," Dawn agreed.

"Okay, so this is especially important for the executive (the dynamic duo of CEO and COO), and is imperative for you, Mark." Adjusting his tie a bit, he turned to me. "Let me explain why. I'll use an example specific to you. Currently, Mark, you have several roles within the company. First, you are the CEO. Second, you are still a 'producer' who sells the product. You might have other roles as well, but these two alone will showcase the concern. In this example," he looked at Dawn, careful not to exclude her from a helpful point, "let's assume that Mark the CEO needs to address an issue with the team. The team members are listening to Mark, but in their minds, they can't figure out who's addressing them: Mark the CEO or Mark the producer? Do you see how problematic this could be?"

"No doubt," I said.

He nodded. "If, for instance, you ask one of the team members to do something, they might have a different response for Mark the CEO than they would for Mark the producer. This gets really concerning when the people on the team feel they're in a no-win scenario. They're supposed to follow a certain process and ensure that Mark the producer follows it also. But if Mark the producer *doesn't* follow the process, how should they respond? Suddenly, they are aware that you are Mark the CEO. Suddenly, that's the hat you're wearing, and they don't want to disappoint you or overstep their perceived limited authority of their role, so they make the mistake of allowing Mark the CEO to not follow the process. It's a tough situation for everyone. Your two different hats signify two different ways they feel they should treat you, but they can't recognize which is which in this situation. Since your default hat is obviously the higher ranking one, the one most feared or respected (depending on the relationship), they defer to the CEO hat and accommodate you at the expense of the process, or the system, or both."

I leaned back in my chair, processing this. "I can see how the multiple hats could send mixed messages ... depending on their perception of the situation."

"Exactly, and that is why whenever someone fills multiple roles within a business, we *always* need to make sure we are conscious of what hat we are wearing at any given time, and what hat we *should* be wearing."

"And that everyone on the team knows how to tell them apart," Dawn added.

"Yep," he said, smiling at her contribution. "Lots of hats to juggle to get clarity, but a day in the life of a business. It's when we jump back and forth between different hats that members of a team can get confused. It's like that shell game where the ball is hidden underneath one shell and then gets quickly juggled around the others. Invariably, we miss where the ball ends up. In business, we sometimes miss the change of hats. We must be aware of which hat we're wearing, but it's even more important to be conscious of which hat the team members *think* we're wearing in any given situation. Clear?"

"Yup." I nodded. "The people on the team need to know which 'Mark' they're dealing with and addressing at any given time."

"I totally get it," Dawn agreed. "There have been times, Mark, when you've been talking to me about some business issue or situation, and it's been like you were wearing both hats at once. I know it's confused *me* at times, so I can only imagine what it does for the team. That said, I'm sure I'm guilty of doing the exact same thing to others as well without realizing it."

I sighed. "I need to really get my head around what you're saying and really think about it."

The captain agreed, and as he continued, I noted sympathy in his voice. "It takes a little discipline to recognize when this two-hat dilemma is happening in any business. Luckily," he grinned crookedly, "I have some ideas to help you with the process. Are you open to hearing th—"

"Absolutely," I replied, not even lettering him finish his question.

He laughed. "Okay, well it involves almost an exaggeration of clarity on two fronts: meeting type and roles represented. First, you have to make sure you have clarity on what type of meetings happen during the day. If you have several types, some of which require you to be in different roles, you need to carefully distinguishes between them. For example, you could have weekly CEO/COO meetings. Within this meeting, you would ensure to only ever wear the CEO hat."

"Makes sense," I said, "but if I *have to* wear two hats within a single meeting? Some other meeting than that one? How do I deal with that?"

"Good question. If you had a meeting during which you're required to represent two hats, sometimes a simple action can help you with the clarity. For example, you could get up and announce that Mark the CEO is leaving, and that Mark the producer is now in the room. That might seem odd or extreme, but it helps the clarity of the organization."

"It's that simple?" I asked.

"Well, simple to understand but more challenging to live on a daily basis within the business. You have to remain consistent, but if you do, the organization will start to speak the same language over time and to recognize the various roles. For clarity, it could be as simple as telling people which hat you're wearing when interacting. You could say, 'I will put on my CEO hat for this one' or 'My CEO hat is off right now, and I'm wearing my producer hat.' Again, this will feel odd at first, but it'll help the organization with clarity a great deal."

I ran my fingers through my hair. "Think I'm wearing my nervous hat at the moment," I said, shaking my head. "Hard to imagine not feeling silly."

He grinned. "It does take a bit to get used to, but your team will help you adopt the approach more and more once they realize it helps them. They'll also pitch in sometimes by having some fun with it. They'll start to ask you which hat you're wearing and will become the mirror for you in terms of which Mark is present in that moment. The organization will have to live with it feeling odd for a while, but eventually, it *will* become part of the DNA of the firm. Then longer term, as you build out each role with a unique individual, your overlap problem subsides. Clear to everyone?"

"Yep," I answered. Dawn nodded as she continued typing furiously.

"Okay, well, not to break the momentum," he said, "but nature calls. Could you direct me to the washroom?"

I did, and once he was safely beyond earshot, I quickly turned to Dawn. "Well, what do you think?"

"Incredible," Dawn gushed. "As he covers these ideas, so many ideas are popping into my head for how we could put these concepts into play as part of the business! I can't stop typing."

"I know," I said. "I had some questions I originally wanted to ask him, but it's flowing so good, I think we should just let it keep going. At the end, if there is time, we can hopefully get those questions in."

I thought about what the captain had told me on the fishing trip about the promise he'd made to his mentor to pay his advice forward. He was delivering on that promise in spades.

CHAPTER THIRTEEN
A DAY IN THE LIFE OF A CEO

After the captain made his way back to the boardroom, he quickly dove right back in. "It occurred to me that I might just be babbling on and not covering the materials you actually want me to cover. If it's okay, though, I thought I would just expand on a few of the concepts we talked about on the boat to give you some more depth. I will keep going until I hear you cry mercy, but make sure that you do if I start babbling. Now, just so I'm not missing anything, is there some specific area of what I shared on the boat on which you would like me to elaborate?"

"First, by no means are you babbling," I said. "Dawn and I were discussing that after you stepped out, and we love this approach. We can always ask questions as we go or at the end if something needs to be further explained or clarified. You should just keep going."

He thought for a moment. "Okay, well, if you like, I could spend some time on your very specific roles within the organizational chart, namely the dynamic duo or executives, the place where the vision meets execution. How does that sound?"

"Sounds good," Dawn answered. I nodded in agreement.

"I want you two to be very clear on the executive roles and their purpose in the business. Although I will focus on each of you one at a time, I think it would be beneficial for each of you to hear what I describe to the other in terms of these key points of each role. By addressing the collective executive, which is you two, it allows you both to fully understand the larger picture of what the other is trying to accomplish. If you're good with that, let's dive into the first role of the business, the CEO, responsible for the vision and direction of an organization."

Although I was excited to hear what he had to say, there was a part of me that was nervous, and the captain picked up on it right away.

"Are you nervous right now or afraid?"

"Both, really. Should I be?"

He shook his head. "The only thing we fear is what we know about ourselves. Mark, what do you know about yourself that's scaring you?"

"I know that I have a long way to go to be the best CEO I can be for this company. The kind of CEO it needs. I'm open to the journey of learning, though. Let's get started."

Dawn was looking at me intently. I don't think she had ever seen me so nervous or uncomfortable. The only consolation I had was knowing that, once the captain was done with me, she was next up. From a comfort level, that switch could not come fast enough for me.

"I'll go easy on you," the captain said, giggling once again. "I think I'd like to try to explain, from experience, what I've seen works best in this role, the sort of attributes that are the most successful, as well as some pitfalls to avoid as you position your mindset for being a CEO. The first attribute is a willingness to trust. You *must* trust your team; you have to trust the processes of the business, and that in the long run, you will be successful by using a trusting approach. You need to believe in the team you've assembled in this business and believe that they are on your team for the right reasons. And what you need to trust the most is your COO. Dawn *must* be at the top of the trust ladder."

He stopped talking and looked at me intently for a moment and then at Dawn. This look seemed to last an eternity before he finally continued.

"Micromanagement has an extreme cost in business, and as the CEO, you *need* to understand this ... better than anyone." He let the words sink in before continuing. "Mistakes happen within businesses. The best-laid plans of mice and men often go awry. But instead of reacting to a mistake by putting into action some ill-conceived plan throughout the organization, it's important to understand what the real mistake actually *was*. In my experience, I have seen that the real mistake is generally just not accepting that mistakes happen sometimes. This is especially true when we're putting in new processes or when people are new to their roles in a business. You need to allow a margin of error before concluding that things are not working and jumping in to fix the problem."

"So if I'm hearing you right," I offered up, "I should just let it happen? My instinct is always to jump the gun, leaving my lane to try to fix the problem. But you're telling me to quit establishing

Band-Aid processes to keep mistakes from happening, interfering with the process. I should just trust Dawn and her team to do their job and be patient with them."

"That's exactly what I'm saying. And yes, I know this approach can seem counterintuitive, but that *is* what I am saying. Too often when we micromanage, we do so because we believe it will be a cost savings in the end, ensuring that mistakes don't happen at all. We make the common mistake of thinking it's better if we just do things ourselves as opposed to allowing others to learn to drive their cars on their own. By micromanaging, we end up costing the firm far more money in terms of lost confidence when people are not allowed to learn and improve within their roles, as well as in real dollar cost to the business. Most people just don't take the time to actually calculate it."

"I remember. Like what you showed me on the boat." I turned to Dawn. "He calculated how much it would cost the business if I took an hour a week away from my own role to basically micromanage someone else's in order to prevent future mistakes. It was a lot." I looked back at him. "This part, though, about just staying in my lane and letting mistakes happen, is still difficult for me to fully buy into. No offense."

I noticed a knowing look on Dawn's face as the captain I were going back and forth. She obviously knew perfectly well how much I interfered, getting too involved in other people's roles and making a mess out of everything, and was clearly pleased that the captain had called me on it on our fishing trip.

"No offense taken," he said pleasantly, looking back and forth between Dawn and myself. "For the record, although this lesson might seem directed at you, Mark, I think it's important to know that it applies to everyone within the business. Everyone needs to trust each other and trust the process in order to get the best possible long-term outcome for the business."

Dawn sighed, nodding. "I get that. It goes for me as well." She looked over at me then. "There are definitely times when I'd like you to just allow me to handle a problem myself, but you want to be involved."

Before I could respond, the captain jumped in. "It is imperative that you protect your lane, Dawn. By doing so, you protect the organization. *Everyone* needs to stay in their own lane, and this is the place the dynamic duo need to reach. Every time you allow Mark to leave his lane, you put the organization at risk in the long term. Are you capable of letting Mark know when he's left his lane?"

"To be honest, I'm not sure," she confessed. "It's not what I'm used to doing, and ... well, it's not what Mark is used to hearing."

"That's true." I sighed. "I guess I need to do a better job of trusting the process, and you specifically, Dawn. Given the way I've been doing things historically, this is going to be a real journey."

"Yes, it will," the captain said. "A journey of positioning this company for long-term success. It starts with your actions, Mark. I need you not only to give the COO title role to Dawn but to give her the autonomy of that role. Can you do that?"

"Autonomy?" Dawn asked.

The captain nodded. "Too often, people are given a title but not the autonomy to really own it and make the decisions that come with it. It's a kind of control kept by the person assigning the roles. They give the person the authority to fill the role but only up to the point where they do not. It's like one of those paddles with a ball attached to it with a string. The ball can only go so far out before it springs back to the paddle. It's a common approach taken by those with control issues."

"He means me," I said sheepishly.

She smiled at me. "I need you to untie the ball, Mark."

"I know. You're right. I've got a lot of soul searching to do about the approach I was using." I sighed yet again. "It's going to be along journey indeed."

CHAPTER FOURTEEN
DECISIONS DISSECTED

The captain must have sensed that it was time to move on to another topic, so he shifted gears. "Let's dive into another attribute. This one centres around decision making and the outcomes of decisions. Way too often, I see CEOs judge their decisions by their outcomes rather than by analysis of the decision-making process. Do you know what I mean by this?"

"I'm not sure I do, actually." I turned to look at Dawn, and she just shrugged her shoulders.

"Well," he said, "let me use a highway analogy for this one."

I grinned and shook my head. "You like your highway analogies, don't you?"

He smiled. "Things happen fast on a highway and sometimes with dire consequences. Lots of parallels to business. So let's say the three of us were standing on the edge of a busy six-lane highway during rush hour. The cars are speeding by, and I suggest that I should attempt to run across the highway to see if I can get to the other side. Obviously, neither of you would think that was a good idea. Nonetheless, I go ahead and run across the highway. By some stroke of luck, or a miracle, I'm able to avoid getting run over and arrive on the other side safely. Once there, I declare that my decision was correct, as evidenced by the outcome, namely my arrival safely to the other side. Thoughts?"

"It was a terrible decision!" I blurted out. "You just got lucky!"

Dawn jumped in too. "It definitely wasn't smart to begin with, so not a good idea, even though you survived."

"Thank you for the clarity and your feedback, both of which help drive home my point. The outcome of a decision, in this case the arrival on the other side of the road, has nothing to do with whether or not it was a good decision. The two are unrelated, independent of one another. As the CEO, the most important part of any decision is to understand the process by which it is made in order to determine if it is flawed or actually makes sense. We need to remove the outcome from that examination. This is important in business but also works in life, by the way. Have you ever heard someone start a sentence with the following phrase: 'See? I told you we should have ...'"

"Many times," I said.

"When the words that follow that phrase are added, what is the overall statement saying in terms of outcome and decision making?"

"That given the outcome, whatever that is, you had made the wrong decision," Dawn replied.

"Exactly. I suspect the people from whom you've heard that saying throughout your life are not the CEOs of any company. Am I right?"

Dawn and I just smiled. "Wow, you must be psychic."

He laughed. "When you learn to separate a decision from its outcome, it helps to separate the emotions from it. This helps you see it more clearly, and people will be amazed at how well you can distance yourself from potentially emotional outcomes. CEOs are often considered emotionless by laymen, but that's not accurate, at least not for most of the ones I've known over the years. It's just that they understand decision-making process at the highest level and don't let themselves buy into outcome-based emotions. It's just another process within a business."

"The word 'process' seems to come up over and over in business, doesn't it?" I observed.

"True, at its core, business only has three parts: product, people, and process. That's a concept that has been around for years, but it's getting more visibility lately. Get these three areas right, and a business will be quite successful and predictable.

"Pause," Dawn blurted out. "Please." She shrugged then. "Sorry, with all the 'P' words—product, people, process, and predictable—I thought I would throw a couple in too. I'm parched. Why don't we take break and grab ourselves a pop ... or a Perrier? There are pastries and peanuts on the lunchroom counter as well."

With a smile, Dawn led us out to the lunchroom, where we could get both beverages and snacks. It felt nice to get up and stretch my legs. *That wasn't so bad,* I thought. The captain seemed to be taking it easy on me, although maybe he was just warming up. I was really glad Dawn was part of our discussion this time and seemed to be very comfortable with it. *It'll be easier discussing all this later this way, going over what we've learned and planning where we're going in the future. It'll l be nice to have her hold me accountable in the future too, if I want to really start changing my approach.* I was confident and thought I could do this.

Probably.

CHAPTER FIFTEEN
ONLY YOUR SHADOW KNOWS

After taking a short break, we all returned to the boardroom and settled back down with snacks and a drink in hand, continuing our discussion right where we'd left off with me getting some pointers from the captain. Although most of his points were directed at me, and to be applied by me in this business, it dawned on me that they had a much further reach. The captain was right. They really did extend far beyond a business setting and had lots of other applications in various parts of our lives.

"The third attribute I wanted to cover for the CEO is what I'll call 'Shadow Casting,'" the captain explained. "The question every CEO needs to ask themselves is: What shadow do I cast while fulfilling this role? Mark, I want you to think about your elongated shadow and what it is telling people about you. Every minute, every hour, and every day, your team, your family, and people in the community are watching you. More specifically, they are watching the shadow that you cast." He looked me in the eye. "I'm sure you feel these eyes on you at times, right?"

"Yes, more and more lately, it seems like the world is watching."

"There is an old joke I heard once, or more like an amusing saying, really: He who lives in a glass house should dress in the basement!' A business is like a glass house. There's a spotlight on the CEO role, or any leadership role for that matter. The role of CEO is really one of servitude, not glamour, status, or limelight. Many who aspire to become the CEO of a business do so for the wrong reasons, pursuing prestige or status, which they believe they'll gain once they reach their destination. They fail to understand that, in this role, your role is actually to serve others and empower them. It's not about you and your glory. In this role of servitude, you will be asked, and expected, to trade off a lot of your own privacy, and you need to understand this going into it. As you undertake this journey, it's important that you understand how to navigate this giant magnifying glass and not get burned."

"Wow," I said, "when you say it that way, it definitely takes some of the shine off the role. Not particularly attractive, is it?"

"Not attractive for those whose who are not clear on *why* they want to take on this role," he countered. "It is a hugely attractive role for those who are wired to serve the company, the team members, and the legacy of the business. It's all about perspective, just like most things are.

"The shadow you cast," he continued, "needs to be consistent over time, and this consistency will drive the calmness of your leadership. Calmness is what's needed by the business itself and those within it. For context, let's look at a couple of actions that might be causing you to cast the wrong shadow at various times during the day. Some of these might seem completely innocent in nature, so we don't realize their impact. They're so ingrained in us and our makeup that we don't consciously even think of them or recognize them when they're occurring. However, if you had a really strong *COO*, that person could help you recognize them more easily. Right, Dawn?"

Dawn just smiled and looked at me. "Yes, I'm sure I could help my CEO shape his shadow."

"Great!" the captain declared. "I want to start this out with the concept of consistency, both in the office and away from the office. Too often, people think that the workday starts at a specific time and ends at another. When, in fact, from a shadow-casting point of view, a CEO is in that role 24/7. By that, I mean that twenty-four hours a day, seven days a week, a CEO is casting a shadow. Well, everyone is really, but we're focussing on the CEO at the moment, as that shadow has the farthest reach. I often see people who act one way at work and then totally the opposite outside of work. This inconsistency is hard to reconcile in terms of figuring out who the person really is. This duality of character is likely hard to manage for the person themself but is especially hard for the people in their lives, who cannot figure them out. Mark, there needs to be only one version of you. Not Dr. Jekyll and Mr. Hyde. Does this make sense?"

I nodded. It seemed clear enough. "I need to strive to be the same person inside and outside of the work environment."

"Right. We rarely think of this in the terms of exposure for your company, but who you are outside of your business is what I call second-level advertising. Let's say your business, and everyone in it, is trying to project an image of professionalism and are consistent in their approach in terms of branding, social media, advertising, and internal imagery. You believe you're doing a good job at it, but on the weekend, you decide to go to the local hockey or football game, and you and some buddies decide it makes sense to see who can drink the most beer. You win the contest but are drunk as a skunk and end up making a fool of yourself in front of some of your clients, who happen to be at the game, and others who don't know you personally but know of your name and your business. Can you see how this extracurricular activity and conduct is not consistent with your brand?"

"Yeah, that wouldn't be good," I agreed. "It would drive people away from my business because of my association with it."

"If this pattern of behaviour persisted, you might find yourself sitting there in your business wondering why the branding and social media isn't driving in more results, when in fact it's you and your conduct that's singlehandedly driving away potential clients who don't want to be connected to that sort of *un*professionalism."

"The world is watching," I said, digesting the truth of his words. "At all times. I'm a walking billboard for my company."

"That is indeed the case," he agreed. "Be consistent in the person you are inside of work and outside. Now, let's shift gears. I noticed you have some framed images throughout your office, with motivational sayings on them."

I nodded, confident in this choice at least. "I feel they help reflect what we believe in within our walls and send a positive message to the team members."

The captain nodded his way through my explanation. "These are commonly used wall decorations throughout offices across the country. They are hung as a reminder of positive messages. However, when I visit an office and see them, most often what they remind me of is the gap between what is written and what actions are actually taking place within that business."

"How do you mean?" Dawn asked.

"Allow me to elaborate," he said. "There are many ways to communicate, but I want to concentrate on three specific ones: verbal, written, and through our actions. Which one of these three communication approaches do you think carries the most weight or is the most effective?"

"Verbal," I quickly announced.

"Actions?" Dawned suggested.

"Give the lady a prize!" the captain declared. "It's a person's actions that carry the most weight. Verbal and written messages can be heard, but actions scream their message. It isn't the messages you communicate verbally or anything you have written on the walls that carry any weight. It is your actions and only your actions that tell the team the behaviour set that is acceptable for this business.

"If you say something and then your actions do the opposite," he explained, "then there is a disconnect between you and your shadow. Words *have* no shadow. Only the person delivering them does, and as such, only your actions cast a shadow. It is our daily actions that carry the most weight in terms of communication. The shadow from these actions can override anything we have ever said. I'm sure you have both seen this in play in your office?"

"Hundred percent," Dawn said. "Way too often, as a matter of fact."

Although I nodded, my mind was searching for examples to support Dawn's obvious confidence in her answer.

"The age-old saying 'Do as I say, not as I do' helps illustrate my point," the captain said. "This saying was likely created out of necessity to remind people to try to do the opposite of following their leader. *As* leaders, we love when people follow us and copy us. It's flattering and feels good. However, when we step out of line, and our actions are not consistent with the message, we create a problem—a problem that we really don't know how to handle. This is where we scramble and start to think that the solution is to remind our followers not to copy our actions but just do as they're told. This is invariably just an excuse because we don't want to take ownership of our actions. When the organization starts to act out on what they have seen, rather than what they've been told, we seem genuinely shocked. Where did this poor behaviour come from? Where did it start? Who taught our team members that this behaviour was okay? These are common questions we throw about. And the answer is a concept we've all known our entire lives: Monkey see, monkey do. Even though we know this intellectually, we cannot help ourselves and continue to set examples that are inconsistent with our words."

"If I am hearing what your shadow is casting," Dawn said with a sly smile, "Mark and I could actually be the problem? If, for instance, we verbally tell our team to make sure they follow a certain process that is important to our company and do not follow it ourselves, we are casting the wrong shadow. It acts as a green light for them not to follow the process either. Right?"

"Precisely." The captain nodded, pleased she understood.

She looked over at me. "You and I are bad monkeys." I laughed, and the captain joined in.

"Okay, I'm a believer," he said. "Going forward, I believe that you both understand that you hold the key to casting only the shadow you actually want to cast."

While I had laughed along with them, I knew very well that Dawn was being very nice to me by choosing not to tell the captain who the real guilty party was. I'm sure he suspected this to be the case anyway. I was definitely the bad monkey, guilty of casting the most inconsistent shadows in my business and doing it quite regularly, as a matter of fact. I needed to improve what I was doing if I wanted to be viewed as a real leader in this organization. Just then, something caught my attention, and I started to giggle internally (at least, I don't *think* I actually let it escape). *You have got to be kidding me,* I thought as I looked down and noticed the snack that this particular bad monkey had brought back with him from the lunch room: a large, fully ripe banana.

CHAPTER SIXTEEN
MY NEW BFF: CANDOUR

I didn't know what was going through Dawn's mind as the captain continued to impart his wisdom, but if it was anything like what was going through mine, then she was just as thrilled that we had found someone who could guide us moving forward in our business with no hidden agenda, with our best interest at heart, and with the wisdom of experience. The fact that the captain was in our office this afternoon, spending this time with us, gave me an incredible feeling inside. The humble gratitude I felt wash over me was something I had never experienced before, or at least not to this extent. I was perfectly content to be a sponge, soaking up all that was offered and hoping the afternoon would never end. Unaware of the emotional impact he was having on me, the captain continued the conversation with the ease of a man who had seen most of what life had to offer and had survived to let the world know.

"Although you have only known me for a short time," he said, "I think you see a pattern in terms of how I deal with any subject, the words I choose to use, and how I work my way to the points I want to make. I call it 'candour' and use it in every aspect of my life."

"Yes, you're very candid, for sure, which I admit I'm not particularly used to."

Dawn smiled. "I like it."

"Does it remind you of a conversation with your BFF?" he asked her.

Her eyebrows shot up in surprise. "Yes, it does, actually."

"Um ... BFF?" I asked.

"Best Friends Forever," the captain said, grinning. "Honestly, Mark, you need to keep up with the times." Dawn laughed, and I rolled my eyes at them both.

Perhaps aware that I was missing the point of this last exchange, he carried on. "Mark, let me help you out and explain my BFF reference. The fourth and final attribute that you need to cultivate as the CEO is candour: the ability to say what is on your mind in a direct way that doesn't offend the person receiving it but instead brings you closer together. A conversation you would typically have with your BFF would naturally be candid. You can say anything to your BFF, and they can say anything to you, because it would never be taken out of context. Everyone would just take it the way it was intended, trusting that it came from a place of love. We must try to replicate this type of safe, BFF environment in the relationships within our business. It needs to become a place where it's safe to have any conversation with anyone, so that we can get to whatever is really at the root of any exchange. We can start this process by just being candid in our approach."

"I don't know, Captain." I suspected he might actually be off the mark on this one. "I don't know if that'll work within our business. I've tried to have some very open, candid conversations, and they generally haven't gone well."

"I think I remember the main conversations you're talking about, Mark," Dawn added. "They really *didn't* go the way you wanted them to, and I had to do a lot of damage control."

"The reaction of others is often what we worry about when we consider this approach," the captain replied. "If you like, I can give you a couple of pointers to help make sure this approach *is* well received and becomes the norm rather than the exception."

"That would be great because this messenger does *not* want to get shot when he delivers his message."

"It's all in the delivery," the captain explained. "There are times when, if the message is delivered with the wrong *intentions*, the messenger *should* be shot."

"Wow. Harsh. But what do you mean by 'intentions?'" I asked. "I would have thought it was only about speaking plainly and making sure your facts are accurate."

"By the reactions you seem to have gotten during those past unfortunate conversations, I suspect that the accuracy of the facts was prioritized incorrectly. The key to candour is to understand the intention, your motivation for sharing your message. If it is only about delivering the facts, and the people receiving it feel like they are not being heard or that you do not have their best interests in mind, then the message will fall flat. Or worse, it will make the receiving party very defensive. Is that what happened in those conversations?"

"Pretty much, yeah."

"As I think of candour," he said, "I am always reminded of a story I heard long ago. It's about an older brother who goes on holiday and asks his younger brother to watch his dog. While he's away on his trip, the older brother calls back home and asks how his dog is doing. 'Your dog is dead,' the younger brother announces. 'What?' the older brother says. 'You can't just tell a person their dog is dead without warning! You have to ease them into it!' ... 'Well how would I do that?' asked the younger brother.

"'You would first say that the dog is on the roof but not to worry,' the older brother explained. 'Then the next time I called you, you'd say that you tried to get the dog down, but it jumped off the roof and broke its leg, but it's at the vet and doing fine.' The older brother continued. 'The next time I called, you'd say that there were complications from internal bleeding, and the dog had passed away. By doing it that way,' the older brother concluded, 'it wouldn't have been such a shock to me. Does that make sense?' The younger brother thought about it for moment and then said, 'Yes, that makes sense.'

"Pleased, the older brother decided to change the subject. 'So,' he asked, 'how is Grandma doing?' 'Well,' replied the younger brother, "she's on the roof.'"

Something about the timing of this joke or his delivery left us both in stitches and broke the seriousness of the mood, allowing us all a chance to laugh for a moment before he brought us back to the subject at hand.

"All right," he said, still smiling at our reaction, "enough of that. The point of that story is that although there is no escaping the fact that uncomfortable subjects sometimes need to be brought up, and facts need to shared, it's all in the delivery. With candour, it's about positioning the people receiving the message so that they can see a clear path to moving forward after the message has been delivered. Your sole motivation must be for the betterment of the individual you're delivering it to. If it is, then that is how it will be received. If your directness is actually about tearing a person down over some mistake or showboating, then it's about you, not them, and it will not be received well. The proper use of candour seems to be a lost art at times, but it's one I believe we need to strive to learn and understand if we want to become effective leaders."

"Well," I said with a smile, "you seem to have mastered it."

"Thank you. It takes time and a consistent approach to get it right, so that when you deliver even a hard message, it is received softly. When I first started using this approach, I was more like a bull in a China shop. With time, though, you get to understand how it can be used effectively. At that point, you'll understand that it should not only be a part of your everyday approach in business but to your life as well."

"I think we both could learn to use this approach," Dawn confessed as she looked at me.

"Well, Mark, that wraps up my thoughts on you specifically and my guidance on being the best CEO you can be. I wasn't too tough on you, was I?"

"Candidly speaking?" I grinned. "I was a bit worried when you started out focusing on me, but everything makes sense, and the advice gives me lots to think about and to strive for as I work on being this company's CEO. It isn't an easy role, for sure."

"No, it's not. It's quite a commitment, but I believe it's a role you can fill."

"I agree," said Dawn.

"Thanks for the vote of confidence, both of you," I said, sincerely humbled and ready for the challenge. It felt good. "Now, let's move on to our next subject of discussion," I said excitedly. "I'm looking forward to listening in on your conversation with Dawn about her journey as COO."

I turned to her, sending her an only mildly sarcastic smile that I hoped conveyed my message candidly: "*Your turn. Good luck.*"

Dawn's return smile looked nervous and not quite so comfortable now that the spotlight would be shifted to her. I wondered how she'd handle it and hoped he wouldn't too rough on her. I was confidant that I'd also be able to glean some insight into how she handled pressure as I observed their interaction. I hoped this would paint a clearer picture of her for me, in terms of this process and how well we would work together going forward. I stated to get nervous as well. I sighed. *Be careful of you wish for, Mark. Sometimes you might actually get it.*

CHAPTER SEVENTEEN

A DAY IN THE LIFE OF A COO

"How are you doing so far?" the captain asked Dawn.

"It's a lot of information to take in, but you make it sound quite simple and understandable. I really can't wait to implement some of the ideas we've covered so far. I'm sure I'm about to get a whole laundry list of new ideas, though, once you take me through your thoughts on the COO role, and specifically me *in* that role."

"I'll try not to make the list too long," he said, chuckling, "but let's get started. So ... I was focusing in the beginning on the dynamic duo of a business, the CEO and COO. These roles are where the vision and execution of a business meet to give us the business outcome, and both are needed, established, and functioning within a business. Let's spend some time on the execution component now, since that's your role. All right?"

"I'm ready when you are."

He nodded and began. "Vision without execution is hallucination," the captain declared. "Do either of you know who this quote is attributed to?"

"No idea," Dawn said. I just shook my head.

"Thomas Edison, so what I'm talking about is not a new idea. It's at least a hundred years old, yet it's still relevant today, and more importantly, it's still not being 'executed,' as evidenced by how most businesses and their operations function. Dawn, since you're the person responsible for overseeing that everything is getting done, you might have the most important role in this business." After a pause to let that sink in, he asked, "How does that statement resonate with you?"

"Well, on the one hand, it sounds like a lot of responsibility, but on the other, I like how it sounds." Dawn grinned at me. "Did you hear that, Mark? I might have the most important role."

"Yes, I heard it … and if the captain keeps pumping your ego, your head might not be able to fit through the door when we leave."

The captain shrugged, nonchalantly. "I'll be sure not to inflate her ego too much. Now, the COO role is about understanding the vision and direction of a company and then operationalizing the work needed to make that vision a reality. It's about coordinating all the steps and tasks required to make sure the work completion matches that pace set out by the CEO. Does that make sense?"

'Yes," Dawn said.

"Now, I want to be clear when I say 'coordinating.' Often people in this role assume that means doing all the tasks themselves, trying to tackle all of them, or at least being a part of them. This approach will lead to them being overwhelmed and burning out. It's really about understanding what needs to be done and then centralizing this information in an easily accessible format. Breaking down each of the initiatives or projects and then timelining this workload. Once you know the projects that you need to tackle, and the deadlines of each, you are ready to take the next steps and break them down further. You need to start outlining the tasks involved within each project and deciding who will be responsible for each of these getting done."

"Wait a second," Dawn said. "Am I not responsible for the completion of all these tasks?"

"You are responsible to seeing they *get* done, but not necessarily responsible for doing each one of them yourself. It is about allocating resources, delegating the tasks to the support team you have around you, as well as any other supports you have access to. Too often, this is where the bottleneck of execution occurs within a company. The workload isn't distributed amongst the support team but instead is held onto by the COO. This approach has two clear concerns. First, it doesn't allow for scaling up the company because the knowledge of the processes becomes proprietary to a single person versus the firm. And second, it does not allow the rest of the team to learn their roles and the responsibilities within them. Did Mark explain to you the lanes of the highway analogy?"

"I think I explained it all right," I said, jumping in.

"Mark did a good job," she said. "But I thought it was about the CEO drifting across lanes."

"Well, it was about that, for sure," the captain agreed. "But it was also about you as the COO making sure all the drivers in the lanes to your right know what they're doing, in terms of their ability to actually drive their cars. When that has been done, they can drive their cars themselves without needing much guidance from you. Although I am addressing both you and Mark, as CEO and COO, there is lots of overlap in terms of the underlying concepts that each of you could apply to both your roles and your lives."

"Okay, that makes sense," Dawn agreed. "It's hard sometimes to allow others to get the tasks done. I just feel like it's quicker to do them myself sometimes."

I laughed at that. "I seem to recall Dawn being quite pleased as she reminded me of my micromanagement and control issues. This might be a case of the pot calling the kettle black. We really are two peas in a pod. The dynamic duo, indeed."

Dawn thought about it for a couple of seconds and then laughed too. "Mark, you might be right. We may be more the same than we are different. We're going to have to learn from each other's examples."

The captain seemed pleased with this exchange. "It'll be great to see each of you support the other and learn from each other as this business grows and develops. Now, let's get back to *why* you feel it's necessary to try to tackle all the tasks yourself. Besides preferring to just do it yourself, is there any other reason?"

She considered for a moment. "I see that some of the other people on the team are busy, so I just take it on myself. I try not to burden them with it when I don't have to."

"I thought that might be your answer, which ties in to the first attribute that I want to cover in *your* role. Usually, as you've outlined, when people see that someone else is busy, they just decide to keep the tasks for themselves. It's not uncommon. They feel it will get done more quickly that way and they won't have to burden others. And this might appear to be a good solution in the short-term, but it will cost time in the long run. Your first attribute as a COO is 'Team Utilization.' Or as I sometimes refer to it, 'Breaking the camel's back.'"

"Interesting secondary title." She looked intrigued.

"It will seem fitting once I describe the scenario. Imagine you are over in Dubai and drive out of the city to the desert. Once there, you come across a caravan with several camels. Each camel has two baskets slung over their backs. Each of these baskets are designed to carry straw. The strongest camel, or lead camel, has their baskets right full of straw, that has been loaded onto it from the big pile of straw on the ground that is waiting to be carried to its destination. The other camels in the caravan have their baskets only partway filled, and some of the others' were empty. It's clear to you that the pile of straw on the ground is larger than the amount the lead camel can possibly carry, so the other camels will need to have their baskets filled as well. How's your visual so far?"

"I can see it pretty clear."

"Good, so ... to your amazement, you sit watching the people continue to fill up the lead camel, ignoring the others. The most startling observation you make is that the lead camel itself keeps reaching down and adding straw to its own back, as if it oblivious to how this will impact him. The other camels watch this, standing by as the lead camel is continually loaded up by people around it and by its own actions. It's clear to you, and even to the other camels, that the basket is overflowing and too heavy, but no one does anything about it. They just kept filling it with more and more straw. Still with me?"

Dawn nodded.

"Finally, after it can no longer take the weight of the straw, the lead camel collapses." After a quiet moment, he looked into Dawn's eyes. "Thoughts?"

"It doesn't make sense. Why would they keep overfilling the camel?" Dawn asked. "And why on earth would the lead camel compound the problem by adding even more weight to its own back?"

The captain didn't answer right away. He just continued staring at her. Finally, it was Dawn who broke the silence.

"I'm the lead camel in this story, aren't I? Mark is the one loading me up, and the other camels are the support team I have around me."

"You're a quick study," the captain declared. "Your role, Dawn, is to understand the load that must be carried and make sure it is distributed effectively. Your first goal, actually, *is* to try to break the backs of each of the camels around you. We want to test run each camel's strength by loading them up. Seems harsh, but we have to determine whether or not they can handle the load. You have to find where their limits are. This approach will only have two outcomes: either they will be able to handle the load, or they will not. Regardless of the outcome, it's a win for the company."

Dawn and I looked at each other then, puzzled, before she spoke up. "Okay, I might be missing something here, but how does them not being able to handle the load represent a win for the company?"

"At first blush, it doesn't seem like one," the captain acknowledged, "but the win is represented by the clarity of the results. If the reason the camel's legs collapsed was because they were unwilling to spread the load, this provides an opportunity to ensure that they understand the 'distribution of workload' approach. *Everyone* needs to learn to distribute the workload throughout the entire caravan, so that everyone is carrying a fair amount of the straw. Make sense?"

"Okay. Yes." She nodded.

He looked over at me then. "And you *want* Dawn to break their backs by distributing her workload rather than breaking her own back by trying to carry too much. I know that it seems counterintuitive to load everyone up, but we need to strengthen them so that they're up to handling the load that the business needs them to carry in order for the company to function at a high level, in order for it to *execute* its primary purpose. We need to gain an understanding of the overall caravan and its ability to handle the loads required by actually testing each camel, even though that means potentially asking too much of them and mistakes happening. Does this make sense to you, Dawn?"

"Yes, I get your point with the visual, and what I need to start thinking about as well going forward."

"Never add more straw to the full baskets that are already sitting on your back when you have other camels carrying baskets that still have room for more."

"Gotcha." She grinned. "I will learn to distribute my straw better so that the lead doesn't keel over."

"Good. Now, if during the process of loading up your other camels, one of their legs give out, it will only be for one of four main reasons: The first is that the load size is too big. We know how to remedy this, simply by distributing some straw to the others. Second, that camel might simply have weak legs, which could be strengthened through training so that they can handle the load the next time it's put on their back. Third, it could be the overall capacity of the caravan itself, which would mean we need to figure out if we have enough camels to handle the load going forward. And finally, if could be the methods we're using to carry the straw. In this case, we could look at ways of making the loads we carry smaller or lighter. In business terms, this means being creative and coming up with better systems, processes, and technology to try to lighten the load on each camel going forward. Is my lead camel still with me?"

"I sure am."

"Great! Now, I want to add one other concept that will support your team and the workload distribution. This one centres around the capacity of any process you put in place. Often, I run what I call a capacity test on a system."

"A capacity test?"

"Yes, a quick test that allows you to examine a process more clearly by scaling it up," the captain explained. "This is a lesson I learned years ago, coincidentally from a gentleman in your industry, as a matter of fact. I was having coffee with Pic, which was his name, and he was describing a situation in his life that had gotten out of hand.

In pursuit of clients, Pic had decided years before to hand-deliver a calendar for the New Year, just prior to Christmas, to each person's home within his client database. He thought it made sense at the time, and it did, in a way.

"However," he continued, "Pic didn't consider the long-term impact of implementing such a system, especially if you added a few years to the formula. He didn't put it to the capacity test, as I would call it. Obviously, at first this new process had the desired effect and endeared him to the clients, driving up the size of his client base. As the years went on, though, you can imagine the time requirement this took to execute. When I sat down with him that day to have a coffee, he had eighteen hundred people in his database. He described to me how his wife and he now had to start on their deliveries of this calendar on the first of December and continue day and night for the remaining days until Christmas. What had started out as a simple idea had now become a curse rather than a blessing."

"Wow. Sounds exhausting," Dawn said, grimacing.

The captain agreed. "He was quite worn out and exasperated that day I talked to him. The real problem was that Pic had failed to do a capacity test on the system he was thinking of implementing. I want you to imagine that whatever process you put in place suddenly has a hundred or a thousand times the volume to be managed. When you add this new load, does the process still work? You can see by my example that this system would not be workable—was not workable, in fact—once the volume got scaled up."

"So we should be test running *all* our systems, in terms of whether or not they still function properly with exaggerated volumes and stress on them. Yes?"

"Yes. Take technology, for instance. That's something that can help scale up an approach so that we can add tremendous volume to it." He shook his head sadly then. "I can still remember being at that coffee place with Pic, looking dejected as he said to me, 'I wish I'd never started handing out those calendars, buddy boy.'"

"I can think of lots of processes that we do as sort of one-offs that would kill us if we had any kind of volume to them," Dawn confessed.

"Well, the clearer you can see the future with that volume, the easier it is to put in place processes that will pass the capacity test both today and tomorrow, which will protect you all the way along. If you realize that a system or process has no scale to it, then you need to start to make changes now. Part of your role is to lay out the foundation of systems and processes that will provide stability for the company against any capacity storm."

"Capacity tests and camels," Dawn said, looking thoughtful. "Interesting concepts."

"Well," I said, interrupting the discussion, "this camel thinks it's time for a water break. Anyone else thirsty from our time in the desert?"

"I could use a cold water," Dawn agreed.

"I'm used to the heat, so I'll take a coffee instead."

As I got up to stretch, I started to think about the volume of work Dawn had been taking on and how she was distributing it amongst the team. I probably really didn't have a clue as to how much straw our business had in its pile.

Dawn really does do an amazing job trying to handle everything and making sure I'm not too involved in it. Obviously, she could share the load better, though, which she acknowledged herself. The last thing this business needs is our "lead" camel going down.

If that happened, I suspected I'd feel exactly how hot the desert we were in truly was.

CHAPTER EIGHTEEN
THE THREE Ps—THE SUSIE RULE

B ack in our seats in the boardroom and time was flying by. The information we'd received was quite plentiful, and I should have been getting tired, but I felt the opposite. Surprisingly, I was feeling very energized and ready to take on the world. I was learning so many new facets of business and how to view and position each of them. The information and concepts seemed to just make me want to dive in more deeply. Although I didn't know for sure, I suspected Dawn was feeling the same, as she'd seemed to fly back into the room, eager to hear more thoughts on her COO role.

"Let's keep going," Dawn excitedly exclaimed, confirming my suspicion.

The captain gave us a big smile and granted Dawn her wish. "Okay, so problem solving is the second key attribute to your success in the COO role. I want to take you through a concept that over the years has helped me understand the components of dealing with the problems that will arise in your role. Problems aren't exclusive to your role and will happen to everyone in the company, but you will, perhaps, come across them more often than most. The approach I am going to take you through is universal enough to be applicable to all people in the company. And another bonus is that an understanding of this concept can be helpful beyond the walls of work and apply to everyday life."

"I am all ears," she replied. I felt the same way but kept it to myself.

"I want you to imagine that someone comes to you with a problem," the captain said, working to paint her a picture. "That problem centres around a single person ... let's call her Susie. I picked that name on purpose, as this was the name of a person I once had to solve a problem with. Dealing with that problem is how I came up with this concept, which I call the Susie Rule."

She nodded. "All right."

"So, Dawn, let's say someone approaches you with a concern, saying that one of the team members, Susie, isn't doing their job right. Too often in this type of scenario, we all just focus our attention on Susie and what she's doing to see if she really *is* doing it wrong. Instead, I want you to break down this scenario into three areas, each of with begins with the letter 'P.'"

I laughed. "Again with 'P' words!"

"That's right, Mark," the captain said. "This concept is also referred to as the 'Three Ps.' The first P of this concept is the *problem*, which is whatever has been brought to your attention. The third concept is the *person* to whom the problem relates. In this example, the *problem* is about the *person*: Susie."

"That's the first and third P, but what about the second P?" Dawn asked.

"Don't worry. I didn't forget the second P. It's actually the most important, though it's often forgotten or bypassed. The second P in this concept stands for *process.*"

"Not *that* word again!" I joked, shaking my head. "We just can't escape it."

"Processes are everywhere in a business, Mark." The captain smiled. "No hiding from them."

"Okay," Dawn said, "so the three Ps of this concept are problem, process, and person."

"That is correct, and in the correct order too," the captain said, nodding.

"The order matters?"

"Yes, it does in this instance. When we confuse the order of these three points, we waste a lot of time in our business. The order matters. Let me explain—or better yet, let's draw this out on a piece of paper. Why don't we do this together, actually? Do you have any paper we can use?"

"For sure," Dawn said, getting up and moving to the cabinet at the back of the room. "Let me just grab a notepad for each of us, and pencils."

Once we were all sitting again, Dawn and I awaited the captain's instructions.

"I always ask people to draw three rectangles across the top of a blank piece of paper," the captain said. "In the far-left rectangle, write the word 'problem.' In the middle rectangle, write the word 'process.' And finally, in the far-right rectangle, write the word 'person.'"

Dawn and I drew our three rectangles across the top of our page and filled them in: problem, process, and person.

"The first rectangle that we have labelled 'Problem' could also reference any concern or issue someone has. Make sense?"

We both nodded in agreement.

"The middle rectangle, in which we put the word 'process,' is really just the detailed way or system we repeatedly use to handle or execute any task. The final rectangle on our page is the person area. Now, when I say 'person,' this could be an individual person, like Susie from our example, but could also be any company, government, or institution. That box should contain the identity or name of whatever entity is the focus of the problem at hand. Do these three boxes and their designated entries all make sense to you so far?"

"Yes," Dawn agreed, and I nodded my head.

"When a concern or problem arises in our business," he said, "or in our everyday life, for that matter, we too often jump right to the person rectangle, bypassing the process one, and this is where the common mistake happens. We need to learn that the order matters. We need to go in order from the left to the right, from problem, to process, and *then* to person. Let me illustrate why the order is of utmost importance."

"That *would* help me get some clarity," Dawn confessed. "It's still pretty fuzzy."

"Okay, so in our example, someone from the team comes up to you with a problem. The problem itself is that they got an angry call from a client who feels that something is wrong with their investment account, which doesn't have as much money in it as they thought it should. This is a very serious concern, given you handle people's money, and you don't want a reputation for anything that isn't completely above board."

"True," I said, jumping in. "We want to maintain a reputation of being proper stewards of people's money, and that can't happen if they think anything is amiss."

"Of course not," he said. "Now, as it turns out, Susie is responsible for sending out account information to the clients. In this case, the *problem* is the client's concern about their money, and the *person* is Susie, who handles the sharing of information about those accounts with the clients. As we explore further, we discover that Susie sent out a flawed investor statement that didn't accurately reflect the client's investment holdings. We conclude that this error is what caused the problem to begin with and why we're dealing with this situation. Too often at this point, people start to formulate all sorts of opinions about Susie and her competence. They start wondering how they're going to handle Susie and even consider firing her. You can see this happening, right?"

"We do jump to conclusions pretty fast sometimes," Dawn confessed.

"But we don't want clients upset either, so maybe that's warranted."

"This may be true. We certainly don't want to upset the client, but the issue with this scenario is that we never stopped at the *process* part of the formula to determine the clarity of that rectangle before jumping right to Susie. That should never happen. To add some clarity, and to serve as a reminder, I'll have you draw a vertical line down the entire page directly between the process rectangle and the person rectangle."

He waited for us to complete this before proceeding. "This line serves as a boundary, reminding us that we *cannot* cross it without first understanding the process behind any problem. We *will* get to the person aspect in the end, but only once we have understood the process involved. My assertion of the importance of this approach stems from the fact that likely around 90 percent of the problems in a business are not really the actual person themselves but instead a lack of clarity regarding the process."

"That's a pretty high number," Dawn noted.

"It is indeed." He nodded. "Most people start with the person as soon as a problem is presented, which is clearly counter to the model."

"I'm guilty of having done this a lot," I admitted.

"You're not alone, Mark," he said reassuringly. "In this real-life example, which inspired the Susie Rule, I discovered that there was a clear process-related breakdown. As it turns out, the company had changed the system of reporting, separating some of the investment accounts in such a way that they no longer appeared on the same statement. The change itself wasn't the real culprit, though. The real *problem* was that the company had failed to train most of the team on this new system—this new *process*. Susie was not made aware of these changes or trained on how to manage them. Using the old format, Susie had sent out an errant statement. If Susie had been trained on this new process, then the situation would have been avoided. As such, the process was the *problem*, not the *person*. In this example, the blame for the training process, or lack thereof, lies fully with the company itself.

"Makes sense," Dawn said. "But what if Susie *had* been trained on the new process but decided not to follow it?"

"Good question. In that case, assuming the company had implemented and trained everyone on this new process, and an errant statement had still gone out, we would be almost ready to cross the line to the person box. To Susie."

"Finally, we get to Susie—wait a minute. Did you say *almost?*"

"I did. We would still have one more step to take in order to understand why Susie had made this decision before we jumped to any conclusions. Ready with your papers again?"

We both nodded.

"I want you to draw three more rectangles, halfway down the same paper, in the same positions as the first ones, with one on the left, one in the middle, and one on the right."

"What about this vertical line we drew down the paper, between process and person?" Dawn asked.

"It's needed in this example as well," he explained. "So both far-right boxes should be separated from the others by the same line. While you are assessing a business situation, and at anytime you feel ready to cross over the line to the person box at the top of your page, we then need to understand what was going through that person's mind. Hence the three new rectangles you just drew. Label the new rectangles 'Clarity' on far left, followed by 'Coaching' in the middle rectangle, and finally 'Conduct' in the last rectangle on the far right."

I did, glancing over to Dawn's to ensure we were both drawing the same thing. "Okay, all good."

Dawn chuckled. "First the three Ps and now the three Cs."

"That's right," the captain said, giving us a smile. "Using these simple words makes it easier to remember the steps. So now that you also have your three Cs on your page, it's important to understand how the Ps and Cs interact. If we ever arrive at the last P box, the one belonging to the potentially problematic person," he smirked at the alliteration, "we still need to understand how much of any situation is actually that person's fault, which we do using the three Cs: clarity, coaching, and conduct."

"So," Dawn said, her brow furrowing slightly in concentration, "even once the process that led to the problem has been examined and understood, or cancelled out as a contributing factor, I still need to understand the three Cs before diving into dealing with the actual person. Do I understand that right?"

"Yes, that's right," replied the captain. "The first rectangle, clarity, specifically relates to the clarity of the person's role. Do they *know* their role within the company? Do they know the steps or tasks that need to be done within their role in order for them to be successful at it? We need to understand if they do indeed understand their role as much as *we* think they do."

"Clarity of role," Dawn repeated, nodding in agreement. "Got it."

"The middle rectangle is 'coaching.' Has the company provided all the coaching needed for this person to be successful in their role? Have they been coached on the tasks that need completion to fulfill their role? These two rectangles, clarity and coaching, now both need to be graded to let us know if the company has provided an acceptable level of support in both areas. We would then write the grade underneath the corresponding rectangle. We should be striving for a grade of a nine out of ten for each of these."

"What if the grade we give the category is lower than that?" Dawn asked.

"Good question," the captain acknowledged. "When we go through this analysis and do the grading, we discover whether or not the clarity of role has been clearly laid out, or the coaching has been adequate. In either case, if clarity or coaching does not have a passing grade, then the company is at fault. It would be the company's responsibility to take steps to make sure these two categories improve to meet the standards the company has set for itself. Until these both are achieving a passing grade, we need not spend *any* time worrying about the third rectangle that factors in her conduct.

"But what if we *know* that Susie's conduct, as demonstrated by her behaviour, actually sucks?" Dawn asked.

"Be that as it may, we need to do *our* job in terms of fully clarifying her role and coaching her within it before addressing her conduct, at least as it relates to the issue at hand," the captain declared. "Only when we have a passing grade in the first two categories, clarity and coaching, can we cross over the line to the conduct rectangle. These first two rectangles detail the responsibilities of the company toward this person. Those are what we can control. The last category, the actual person and their conduct, we cannot control. Those are Susie's responsibility."

"That seems a little off," Dawn said, challenging him on this point. "If, based on what we discovered by following the initial first steps, examining the problem and the process, we have figured out that the problem actually *is* Susie, why do we need to take these other steps too?"

"To prove that the problem is *her* poor behaviour and not our own. By following these steps, in this order, we confirm that our clarity of role and coaching processes are strong. We must ensure that we don't jump the gun and get rid of Susie only to discover that the real issue was our own company, and more specifically, our approach to 'clarity of role' and coaching. If we don't examine these areas when issues arise, and discover what we need to correct or improve, we can't fix our issues. Susie just gets fired, and then the next person to take on her role will walk right into the same situation with the same results. By skipping this self-examination, we are just setting the *next* Susie up for failure."

"Okay," Dawn said, raising her hands in surrender. "Okay, I get it. That does makes sense."

The captain nodded, taking a sip of his coffee before continuing. "All right, so ... once we complete grading ourselves on these two categories, it becomes easy to see how to deal with Susie. If it turns out the company failed to give her proper coaching or clarity in her role, then we would address it. Likely Susie's conduct will improve once the clarity and coaching improve, which they will thanks to our new focused awareness of the *need* for improvement. If, on the other hand, it turns out that it was Susie's conduct and behaviour all along, then she will need to make a choice about how *she* plans to improve herself, either working her way further into the company by addressing her own flaws or working her way directly out of it."

Dawn sighed. Shaking her head, she unscrewed the cap of her water bottle and took a sip. "Wow. That's a lot of steps to take approaching one little problem"

"It seems like a lot, I know, but this will quickly become second nature to you," said the captain. "And it will protect everyone from spending time and energy on the wrong things. It is a repeatable approach that can be undertaken very easily. I'm sure you can think of some situations where this approach could have saved you a lot of time."

She had to admit that he was right on that one. "There's quite a few that come to mind, actually."

"Me too," I said, "both in business and in my personal life."

"Believe me, the Susies of the world will thank you for taking responsibility and learning these concepts. By doing so, you keep people employed who should be kept when the cause of certain problems actually has the company's fingerprints all over it. Your company and team will also thank you for using a process that will be clear to everyone and ultimately remove people who truly have the wrong behaviour set." The captain smiled at each of us in turn. "I know. Lots to think about."

My head was already spinning with everything we'd just learned, but he wasn't done.

"Welcome to the trials and tribulations of running a great business. I know it can appear daunting, but having clear processes will be worth it. This is where you really earn your titles within the company. Remember what Winston Churchill once said: 'The price of greatness is responsibility.'"

Responsibility, I thought. *There sure is a lot to being a leader in a business. I can't believe I thought that owning and leading a company was going to be a piece of cake. I wonder what Dawn's thinking right now.*

It was appearing more and more that if we were going to add the most value to the business, we had better buckle in for a long journey. *That must be the price of greatness.* It was a price that Dawn and I would need to become comfortable paying.

CHAPTER NINETEEN
TIME IS A FRIEND OF MINE

After yet another short break, we settled back down in our seats around the boardroom table, and I glanced up at the clock. It was getting pretty late in the afternoon. The captain seemed bound and determined to get through all the items he had in his mind, though, wanting to ensure we got the most out of our afternoon with him. I wondered if his seemingly endless commitment to helping us was common for him or if it had something to do with a lingering feeling of obligation he had for my father. In the end, though, it didn't matter. The amount of material he had already provided us with, if implemented to its fullest, would take us through the next year at least, if not several, and help us lay the foundation of the business, with clearly defined roles for both of us.

I had attended seminars that lasted days at a time, looking for ideas on business and just simple guidance. If I added up all time and dollars I had invested over the years in business courses, seminars, and educational events, I suspect its collective value would pale in comparison to what we'd received so far today for free. The captain seemed to understand how to make the abstract business concepts so concrete that it was like we could touch and feel them. And he could obviously chat forever on the subject of business, and Dawn and I were happy to benefit from this fact.

"Okay, Dawn, the last attribute that I want to want to discuss with you today before I go is the most precious piece of information I will have delivered today. And although I am addressing this specifically to you as the COO of the company, this is applicable to you both. This last area of focus is on the subject of time. I feel that what I'm about to discuss is something that is incredibly important for you both to embrace.

"So," he ginned at her, "even though this is your attribute, Dawn, and I really need you to pay attention, I will do something unusual here and address Mark the CEO primarily, using him to initiate and illustrate the attribute in question. All right, so to kick this off, I'm going to ask you a question, Mark. What is your relationship with time?"

A few possible responses flitted through my mind, but none seemed to make any sense. Finally, I shrugged. "I have no idea what you're asking me."

He chuckled. "Right. Okay, so is time a friend of yours or an enemy?"

"Sounds like a question for a philosopher, not financial advisor." I shook my head, fully aware of my own limitations. "I have no idea."

"That's not uncommon, really, but it *is* problematic. Your relationship with time is one of the most defining relationships you will have as the CEO of your firm," he declared definitively. "This relationship will have some of the most polarizing extremes to it. Time will be a friend when you respect it and your worst enemy when you do not.

Your role as CEO is to understand this relationship and make time a friend of yours as often as you can."

I looked over at Dawn, and she was as intrigued by this as I was, though she still looked nearly as clueless as I felt.

"We only have a finite amount of time on this earth," the captain explained. "This allotment of time is precious and should never be taken for granted. Every day, we must choose how to divvy up this time and allocate it out to all of our pursuits in life. In business, just like in life, our decisions on how we choose to use our time are the key to success. Too often, when I meet with the leaders within their businesses, they have no idea of the importance of time, or any other key component, in their success formula.

"I want you to think of the highway analogy we discussed both here and on the boat," he continued. "I want both of you to visualize the traffic moving in unison at the sort of speeds it normally does on a highway. Again, remember this represents how your business is moving. Suppose our goal was to move the business along at a steadily increasing pace. What would the ramifications of this goal be to the drivers, your team, on the highway?"

"I suspect that if we got going too fast, those drivers that couldn't keep up would have to take an exit," I offered.

Dawn nodded. "And some cars might not be designed to go that fast, so this could lead to mechanical problems."

"Yes, both of those are true," the captain agreed. "That truth leaves us with a dilemma: Do we increase the pace of the business or choose to keep it moving more slowly?"

"Slower seems like an odd goal for a business," I said, "and counterintuitive."

"Perhaps," he answered, "but the slow pace will accommodate those that don't like higher speeds or are driving a car that isn't roadworthy for going too fast."

I shook my head. "I still think we should keep moving faster and just find drivers and cars better suited for the speed we need to travel."

As soon as the words slipped out of my mouth, what I'd really just said suddenly dawned on me. I realized what that approach would actually mean to our business and the people in it who were lagging behind. I must have had quite the look on my face because the captain zeroed in on me.

"What are you thinking, Mark?"

"I think my own statement just provided me with the answer to your question, and I'm not sure I like what I heard," I confessed. "We *haven't* been pushing the pace in this business, primarily because it might mean leaving some people behind. I must have known that intellectually, but it just sunk in now."

Dawn just stared at me, trying to digest my revelation. The captain broke the silence that followed with his own thoughts.

"Your job as the CEO is to respect time enough to push the pace of the organization. Dawn's role as the COO is to ensure that we have the right people and processes in place in order to keep up with the pace you set. If we don't have the right people in place, then we need to *get* them in place. When we hesitate to push the pace of a

company because we're worried someone cannot keep up, then we are disrespecting time. Have you ever kept someone in the company even though you knew they couldn't keep up?"

Dawn and I looked at each other. We both knew one person who had been slowing down the pace of the business for a while now.

"Yes," Dawn said. "We have someone right now who's been struggling with the pace of changes being made. Mark and I have disagreed on how to handle the person, so she's still with the company."

"Let me guess," the captain said, nodding. "This is a long-term employee, someone Mark originally hired. He thinks you should keep this person, and you think they should go. So the two of you are left at an impasse, and in the meantime, the business sits in limbo, waiting for direction."

Dawn smiled, looking shocked, then turned to me for a moment before looking back at the captain. "Give this man a prize!" she said, grinning. The captain laughed, appreciating her turning that back on him. "Mark feels that we should keep her because she's been with him for a long time."

"And whose lane does this decision fall in?" asked the captain.

"It's Dawn's lane," I replied. "Obviously." I shook my head. "How come when you say it, I can see it so clearly, but when I'm dealing with it on my own, it isn't so clear?" I sighed heavily. "As much as I hate to admit it, my car definitely veers to the right."

"Sorry, Mark, but this is a great example of giving Dawn the role but not the autonomy. Not allowing her to drive in her lane, on her own, is slowing down the company. She needs to just solve the problem and get someone in that role who *can* keep pace with the business. Now, I'm going to ask you something else. In this example, is time a friend of yours, Mark?"

"No. It's not. I am clearly disrespecting it," I reluctantly replied. "I have to allow the pace of the company to increase and ensure that I'm not building barriers to that."

"You're right," the captain said, nodding slowly. "You do. Most of us worry more about disrespecting people, so we avoid dealing with this sort of problem. Now, Dawn, how is *your* relationship with time in this example?"

"Not good," she confessed. "By me not removing Mark from my lane, I'm not dealing with things *I* need to deal with and actually wasting time. Truth be told, even if he was not in my lane about this issue, though, I might still hesitate to do what I need to do, knowing it would be a very tough conversation to have."

"This avoidance approach that the both of you are choosing to participate in has two very distinct parts to it," he said. "Both of these parts clearly help push you, the executive branch of this company, down the path of disrespecting time. The first part is that when we do not quickly address the issue of people who are not aligned and cannot keep up, what we are in fact doing is disrespecting the pace of business. What pace really is can be described as the *time* it takes to execute its work. Its purpose. Not allowing the business to continue to execute at a faster and faster pace is an example of respecting its time. If we slow the business down for the wrong reasons, then we're not using time wisely. Does this make sense to both of you?"

"Yes," we replied in unison.

"Often, we take this approach because we think the business doesn't have a voice and does not hold us accountable for our avoidance of a situation. Imagine, for a minute, if the business did have a voice. What do you think it would say about you both slowing down its pace because you're uncomfortable with having a necessary conversation?"

"I suspect it would be a candid conversation, for sure." I could almost hear it speaking to me in the captain's voice. "The business would be telling us to stay in our lanes, push the pace, and make sure we have people aligned to this goal."

"Exactly," he said. "I'm curious what your response to it would be."

I sighed. "I suspect it would be another uncomfortable conversation where I have a hard time articulating what really needs to be done." I sighed. "I struggle a lot with this part of the business."

"Mark," Dawn said, "I can handle the people we have on the team." She looked me square in the eye then before continuing in an emphatic tone. "I can handle all the things in my lane *and* in the lanes to my right. You just have to trust me, trust the process, and truly allow me to do it."

I nodded, finally really hearing her. "I guess I just need to put down my hammer and nails."

Dawn frowned at that, looking puzzled.

"Sorry. It's that the ABC thing I told you about at our Monday meeting. I was being a barrier-building CEO, and I have to stop doing that: building barriers to our success. It's about time for me to just let you drive your own car and handle the operations of this business."

"Good stuff!" the captain said, smiling and rubbing his hands together. "All right, now that that's settled, the second part of disrespecting time is something we've already been talking about: avoiding the tough conversations we know we should have. It is within this struggle and avoidance that the most egregious of all the time-disrespecting offences occurs. When I think about this, it actually stirs up lots of emotions within me, so I'll try to move through it quickly. It raises my blood pressure if I focus on it too long."

Both Dawn and I could see this subject matter meant a lot to him and shared a look that seemed to promise that we'd help him get through it without too many interruptions.

"This lesson is seared into my heart and started for me from the most sobering set of circumstances," he said in a voice that made it clear it came right from his heart. "It was when my Uncle Joe was on his deathbed, dying of cancer, and together we were staring out the window from his palliative care unit. It was a fall day, and the leaves were blowing around out on the hospital lawn. We were both quietly watching this typical fall day unfold when Joe said something that struck me as incredibly profound. He said, quite simply, 'I wish I could be outside now.' That was it. That's all he said. Then two days later, he passed away."

We could see that he was deep in thought, momentarily transported back to that time. We let the silence linger, while in my mind, I was busily trying to piece together the connection of his uncle's words to the conversation we were having about time. The connection soon became clear.

"Those words from my uncle always remind me that we have only so much time before we're on our *own* deathbeds." The captain seemed to be staring off into the distance as he spoke, his voice quiet but firm. "And at that moment ... what would we all give for another hour? Another day or week of life? It is only during that moment in time, with our fate staring us directly in the face, that we start to truly realize what each moment of time is worth in our lives."

He looked up at us then, shifting his focus back and forth between us. "And yet, when we are dealing with people who we know clearly do not fit into the long-term alignment of our business, we choose to disrespect *their* time ... by not having a conversation with them that would set them free—free to pursue the destiny that awaits them somewhere else, some place where they *can* find their alignment and harmony."

As he continued, he began tapping the end of his index finger on the tabletop as if to drive each point home. "We do not have the moral authority to make choices on how their time will be spent ... only *they* can decide what it should be used for. But instead, we withhold from them a key piece of information that would likely change their choices, their destiny, at that very moment ... and likely for the better. Their future with the company has already been decided, but no one has let them know. The actual conversation, a life-changing one at that, has just not been executed ... for all the wrong reasons."

I could see the passion and conviction in his words. He truly believed we were doing a disservice to anyone by not letting them go, and in a timely manner, as soon as it became clear that they were not part of our future. And it was clear that he was right.

He shook his head. "We fear that we will upset them, or that they won't land on their feet, so we let these thoughts freeze us in place and keep us from doing what we should be doing. And none of those freezing thoughts are rooted in fact. Look at all the people in your lives, everyone you've known. Have you ever known anyone who had a change in their lives, by their choice or the choice of others, who hasn't end up better off in the long run? In one way or another, at least?"

Silence fell as we both tried to come up with an example. There were lots of short-term ones, but in the long run? I personally couldn't.

Finally, Dawn shook her head. "I can't think of one on the spot."

"Me neither."

"I'm not surprised," he said. "Invariably, when we go through the various contacts in our lives, it's hard to find examples of people who are truly worse off after a change, at least not once the dust finally settles. Yet we fear change in general and making a change that involves people in our business even more so. Well, it's time we got comfortable with these tougher conversations. Do you agree?"

Dawn and I nodded in agreement.

"Dawn," the captain turned a bit in his chair to address her directly, "time needs to become a friend of yours, and you *must* be comfortable with what your friend brings to the table. This is the last attribute of your role, Dawn. Time *is* a friend of yours. Embrace it so that you can allow your people to find a new path, if one is needed ... a path that adds to their lives and the world in general, rather than leaving them stuck somewhere they do not belong."

The dots were connected more clearly for me with every word he spoke. I turned to Dawn and saw her nodding. I think we both knew what out next course of action would be once we'd had a chance to debrief on this last attribute.

CHAPTER TWENTY
HELLO GOODBYE

As we were saying our goodbyes to the captain, a feeling akin to panic came over me. What was going to happen once the captain was gone? It seemed we'd just said our hellos, and we were already at the goodbye stage. I don't know why I felt this strongly, as I felt confidant that we were going to be able to take his advice and put it into action.

Once exchanging a few pleasantries, and assurances that I would pass along another hello from him to my parents, he wished us luck and took his leave. It was now time for Dawn and me to step up and guide this company. We had all the information we needed to start the process of working together with a singular purpose and direction. I don't know if it was because of the sheer volume of information, but at that moment, I was drawing a blank in terms of what our first steps would need to be. I almost felt like chasing after the captain, screaming for him to come back, but I controlled myself, recognizing that this was ridiculous. Dawn looked over to me then and smiled reassuringly, which melted away the momentary fear.

"Shall we debrief for a couple minutes?" she asked.

I knew that once I talked to Dawn, I would have a clearer picture of what was needed in terms of our plan of attack. We settled back down in the boardroom, where Dawn was the first to start talking.

"What an incredible afternoon!" she said excitedly. "Better than I ever could have imagined. I can see why your fishing trip got you so excited that you lost sleep."

"Now you know what I was feeling," I said. "He really makes it sound so easy and straightforward. Like it should only take us a few minutes to put this all into play, but I suspect there's lots of work that really needs to go into this. Do you think we're up for the challenge?"

"I know we are," Dawn declared confidently. "As long as we hold each other accountable, we'll be able to knock off each point in terms of trying to make these lessons and processes part of the DNA of our team and company going forward. Are you having doubts?"

My head bobbled from side to side a bit, acknowledging my uncertainty but determined not to let them win. "Not exactly. At my weakest moments, I likely will have some doubts about our ability to make it happen more than the advice itself, but overall, I think this is just what we need for our company. Why don't we each take some time to soak it all in, put our thoughts down on paper, and then compare notes so we can put our heads together in terms of a plan of attack. How about we let it percolate for the rest of the week and over the weekend and then meet on Monday to discuss and establish our plan."

"Makes sense," Dawn agreed. "It was a lot to digest, and I could use the time to gather my overall thoughts. Monday works great for me. I'm looking forward to it."

I spent the rest of the week, between appointments, thinking about everything the captain had said. I paid special attention to the team and how they functioned together in various situations. I could see lots of areas that we could improve on going forward and how the application of the knowledge the captain had imparted could be integrated. I noticed that Dawn was also observing the team more intently. It was almost as if I could see the wheels turning in her brain. I knew that Monday's meeting was going to be interesting, comparing notes and seeing where we both stood. I was just excited for the weekend to come so I would have time to write down my thoughts from the week more fully.

When it arrived, I decided to spend some time on Saturday morning in my home office, putting my thoughts down on paper. Before starting this process, I thought I would reach out to my dad for a quick call.

"Dad," I said when he picked up the phone, "I just wanted to give you an update on how the latest meeting with the captain went."

"Hi, Mark. I was wondering how that turned out," he replied. "I figured you would give me an update when you could. So better or worse than the fishing trip?"

"Better. Dawn was blown away by him, and he did an incredible job of laying out his concepts for both of us. We're both putting our thoughts together from the meeting and will compare notes on Monday morning. I'm super excited where this might take the company."

"I'm glad he did a good job for you two," he said. "At least your old man has some good advice to guide you with, right?"

"Yes, this time you hit a home run," I said, smiling and happy to acknowledge his input. "I really appreciate you doing that for me."

"I've always wanted to see you succeed—in everything, really—but your business too, so I knew the captain would provide you some good perspectives and ideas on how to go forward. I'm just glad I could help. Now it's your turn to put his advice into play and lead your company where it needs to go. I'm sure you'll do a great job!"

"Thanks, Dad. I'll do my best and let you know how it all turns out."

With that, I told him I needed to get to it; we said our goodbyes, and once I was off the phone, I dove right into sorting out all the information and ideas that the captain had walked me through. I decided to break it down into manageable chunks that seemed to make sense to me. Hopefully, it would make sense to Dawn too. I started with my role as CEO and broke this down into the key attributes the captain had outlined: trust, decisions versus outcome, elongated shadow, and finally, candour. From there, I decided to do the same layout for Dawn, the COO: team utilization, the three Ps, and time.

Before I dove any deeper into each of these attributes, I decided to put down some thoughts that I felt were more about the company itself than any individual role: seeing through the business's eyes, CEO versus ABC, using words that unify a team versus dividing it, micromanagement costs, lane clarity, and organizational clarity.

I sat back and looked at the key areas I had material for and knew I had my list for Monday's meeting. I just needed to add some more context so I could arrive to it feeling well prepared. As I looked it all over, I started to wonder what points were going to be on Dawn's list, and whether or not we would be aligned in our thoughts.

Monday could not come quick enough.

CHAPTER TWENTY-ONE
COME TOGETHER

When Monday morning finally arrived and I headed to the boardroom, Dawn was already sitting at the table with her supplies, a laptop opened in front of her, and a coffee. It appeared she'd gotten there early and was eager to go.

"All set?" I asked her, fully understanding that she was likely more prepared than I was.

"Can't wait," she replied. "I have lots of ideas that wouldn't let me relax all weekend, so I have to confess that I've actually 'been set' for a day or two."

"It should be a good discussion then," I replied with a smile. "How should we start this?"

"Why don't we each give an overview of the highlights or key take-aways from our time with the captain?" Dawn offered up. "You start."

"Sounds good," I replied. "The last couple weeks, and our meetings with the captain, has really got me thinking about the areas our company needs to improve on to be successful. Not that it was going terribly for the company, but I think we could do and be so much more. I think I'd personally like to concentrate on the first points about myself first. What I mean is that I've finally recognized that the old me wasn't helping our journey to success. It became increasingly apparent to me every time the captain would point out some new idea or concept that my understanding, as well as my actions in the past, weren't even in the ballpark. I took some time to write down some key points that I want to share with you about my CEO role and what I want for it going forward."

Dawn smiled, probably enjoying that, without actually saying it, I was eating some humble pie, and that this would ultimately benefit the company and myself in the long run.

"I wrote down four Attributes of a CEO that I want to make sure I start living, and I'm sure I'll need your help holding me accountable to them." I looked up from my notes and saw her nod of encouragement to proceed.

"The first attribute is trust. I realize that I've done a poor job of believing in you and trusting you in your role. As I look beyond you to the overall team, my trust levels drop significantly. No one on the team did anything to truly warrant that lack of faith; it was just me thinking or assuming they couldn't possibly care about the business as much as I do. This led me to micromanage and basically impair our company's true pace. I need this to change, and it will be starting today. You now officially have the COO role within our company, and I will respect you in your role. Furthermore, I will trust that you can operate in your lane and be very good at it. You now also have the full autonomy of the role going forward. You can oversee all manpower and decision related to the manpower within the firm and have my full support. How does that land with you?"

"It lands very well and thank you," she said, and then announced confidently, "I accept it and will do a great job for the business in this role."

I nodded, pleased by her attitude, and went on. "The second attribute is 'focusing on decisions versus outcome,' and I want to do a good job at this. Too often, my focus has been on the outcome rather than on the actual decision-making process. I've been looking at that all wrong. Going forward, I will only use the outcome to quickly test my decision-making process to ensure it is solid and not flawed. I will stop looking through the eyes of the outcome in terms of regrets of any decision. Does that make sense?"

"For sure!" Dawn nodded. "Sounds great!"

I gave her an apologetic look then. "I have often been the worse culprit when it comes to not following the systems you've set out for the company. This leads me to the third attribute that the captain brought to my attention: shadow casting. I am going to be more conscious that as CEO I cast my shadow over the whole team, and this shadow better be reflective of the role model I want to be. I'm going to start leading by example, making sure that my actions are consistent with my words, and that neither contradict the processes and policies of the company. I want to work on being the role model that's needed for both this company and the team, in terms of my conduct."

She seemed very pleased about this one. "The team definitely needs this from you and will greatly appreciate it. It will also take a load off of my plate in terms of any double standard that has been perceived in the past. Thank you."

"You're very welcome. Okay, so the final attribute I want to address is candour, and specifically, candour between the two of us. I want our level of candour to become the envy of other businesses. I want all the feedback you have to share and for you to be perfectly honest with me, not holding anything back. I need to hear your views and want it to be unfettered. And right here and now, I am making a commitment to this company and to you, as my COO, to become the CEO this company needs and the one you deserve to work beside going forward." I fiddled with my notes, feeling a bit shy about my proclamation. After a moment, I glanced back up at her. "That wraps up my initial thoughts around my role as the CEO."

"Wow," she said, shaking her head and obviously impressed. "That was some way to kick off this meeting! I can't wait to see you actually live these attributes and support you as you grow and learn."

"I am going to need your support, for sure."

"Well, you have it, unconditionally." We nodded at each other, and then she continued. "Why don't I take you through my thoughts on my COO role. You might find it amusing to know that I laid it out virtually the same way you did. Two peas in a pod."

"A dynamic duo in a pod."

She giggled at that, then cleared her throat and got back to business. "I have to start out by saying that I spent a lot of time thinking about all the things the captain talked about at the meeting. I especially took to heart his thoughts about my role and its attributes. We all want to add the most value to a company, but a lot of the time, it just seems like things are getting in the way of everyone being the best team members they can be."

"I hear that," I said, nodding.

"I thought about the camel story a lot, and how I might be guilty of carrying too much straw and not letting go of some of it very easily," she confessed. "The COO's first attribute, team utilization? I want to put that in place right away and make sure I'm really living this one. There's no reason we can't have everyone completely clear on their lanes and make sure they're given a chance to handle the load that's required of them. We need to get everyone up to speed in terms of where we're going and allow them to drive their cars the way they're designed to be driven."

"Absolutely."

"This leads me into the second attribute I outlined," she said. "The Susie Rule is going into effect right away. I'm going to use the three-Ps system to ensure we have organizational clarity in terms of how we react to problems or concerns. We're definitely burning too much time pointing fingers instead of hanging out in the process room and trying to get clarity. We have to make sure everyone is clear on their roles and are fully trained, coached, and supported. This will give the organization the opportunity to excel. There's no reason for our company not to ensure these areas always get a passing grade. So going forward, it will."

"That'll make a big difference to everyone who works here, I'm sure."

"I am glad you think so," she said. "It's evident to me that we need to make sure everyone who works here is fully on board. In terms of our problematic team member," she glanced at me to be sure I knew who she was talking about, and I nodded, "I want to respect time, my third attribute, enough to handle this problem. The way I plan to handle it is to be sure we have first offered her all the clarity, training, coaching, and support she might need. Through this process, I will not only be outlining her role but also the expectations of the firm, so there is no confusion. If, through this process, we come to the realization that she really is a poor fit with this business, then we will be parting ways with her. But first, I want to be absolutely sure that her pace has nothing to do with any lack of clarity, clear process, or support that might have been problematic in the past. I will execute this approach right away and conclude the process as quickly as possible in order to respect her time, should we need to terminate her. How does that sound?"

"I can live with that for sure," I said. "It sounds like a very fair approach for everyone."

"All right, well, that's my list of attributes for my role, and for how I plan to incorporate them. Do they make sense?"

"Absolutely."

"So," she said then, sounding a bit hesitant, "I also have some thoughts or truths about the company that I would like to share with you."

"Truths?" I asked.

"Well, for lack of a better word," she answered. "I've made up a list of truths, or values maybe, that we can share with everyone, maybe posting it in the community areas and try to live by, every day, within the company. The first one I came up with is called 'Harmony on the Highway.' I want everyone to understand this analogy and make sure they are clear about which lane their car operates in. If we are all aware of this and use this analogy with everyone, then I believe we can get the lanes clearer and clearer, with everyone more able to drive in their own lanes. Does that make sense so far?"

"Yep. It does. Please, keep going."

"Okay, the next one is 'Organization Optics,'" she explained. "We need a clear organizational chart, available for everyone, so we can all clearly see how and where they fit and how we are going to build this business together. I don't think we should ever have anyone on this team who doesn't have a clear picture of the team itself from an organizational perspective."

"I totally agree. Great idea." I was really impressed with everything she'd come up with and realized I'd been doubting her for absolutely no reason for a long time. "Do you have more?"

"Yes, the third one I came up with is called 'We Words.'" Dawn glanced up at me from her notes. "Is that too goofy? I want us all to use words that emphasise that we're a *team* here. Inclusive words that bring us together with no one feeling alienated. We can call it something else if you like."

"Well, a *boss* might think 'We Words' is too goofy," I said, smiling, "but your CEO doesn't. This is a very important area and something to which we should all hold ourselves accountable. I really like this one. Great idea."

"Excellent," she said, grinning and visibly relaxing. "Well, those are the only truths or values I came up with, but I'm sure we can think of others to add as we go along."

"I actually have a couple more for the list that we could add right now. As I had the opportunity to spend more time with the captain than you did, there are a couple more that jump out at me. The first one would be 'You Don't Spell CEO with ABC.'"

"I don't get it." She looked puzzled.

"I think it came up at our group meeting, but we didn't really get into it too deeply. The captain told me that a CEO can sometimes actually end up being an ABC, as in 'A Barrier-building CEO,' one who gets in the way of processes and the pace of the business by their actions, beliefs, or biases, instead of supporting them and acting in a way that actually helps the business, or its people, to succeed. We can add context to this one with our staff in the beginning, explaining it to them, and then I can work to model it as we move forward."

She grinned. "I like that one." I watched as she added it to her list, typing it quickly into her word document. "Do you have any more?"

"Yeah, the other one is 'The Business's Eyes First,' which is a bit trickier to explain but centres around my role, reminding me that I should always be acting as the eyes of the business, looking at choices through its eyes before making any decisions that might impact it, working always for its best interest rather than my own."

She considered it for a moment and then shrugged. "It seems a bit abstract to me, but I'll trust you on that one. I'm sure it'll start to make sense as we go along. If it came from the captain, I have no reason to think it isn't sound." She typed it in.

"Anything else?"

"Just one more," I said. "This one might be along the same lines as your 'Harmony on the Highway,' but I think it should stand alone: 'Micromanagement Has a Cost.' I want to be sure that we *all* know that we need to allow others to execute their roles, even though that means that mistakes will sometimes happen. We should just think of those mistakes as opportunities to learn. I think this is an important one, and one I'm sure I'll need to be reminded about."

"It certainly is," Dawn agreed, "and you certainly will." She smirked at me, and I started to laugh quietly, enjoying our new candour. "I think we've come up with a good start on this list of truths or values. I can't wait to make the team aware of them, and more importantly, to make sure we adopt them in our everyday lives here."

"I couldn't agree more. If we were to both take steps to really live our roles and the truths of the company, I think we should see some incredible changes to our path going forward."

"I am so excited to see where this could go," Dawn stated and then leaned back in her chair, smiling at me. "It's nice to see us come together on a common approach that will be clear to the team."

"It feels right, doesn't it? A great starting point to build on."

———

For the rest of the meeting and throughout the week, we continued to add items and context to our lists. By the following week, we were satisfied with where we'd gotten with it, so we unveiled it to the team and were well on our way to having clarity in both our business and our roles. Our ship was no longer adrift.

From then on, it would be one that was guided, candidly, by the captain.

CHAPTER TWENTY-TWO
MAKING TIME FOR THE CAPTAIN

It sure wasn't fishing weather when Dawn and I pulled into Waterton Park in early December. All the hustle and bustle of the summer tourist season was long gone, and the park was a lot quieter. It still offered a certain beauty in its solitude, though, even this time of year. The snow had laid a white blanket on the ground, though we could see that there was still plenty of wildlife out and about as we entered the park and drove toward the townsite, spotting furry animals, large and small, crossing clearings and scurrying around through the nearly naked trees, as well as the familiar V formation of Canada Geese making their way steadily toward warmer climates. Between the snow, the mountains, and the animals, the day was magical. I had spent part of our drive extolling the beauty of this location to Dawn, who had never visited it, so I was pleased that she didn't seem disappointed.

"This place is incredible!" she said for the third or fourth time. "I can't believe the number of deer and elk just wandering around the town."

"Yeah. Easy to see why the captain loves it here."

After some snooping from my dad to ensure that the captain would likely be home, Dawn and I had decided to make a surprise trip to see him. It had been nearly four months since he'd come for the visit to our office, and this time we wanted to go to him. We pulled up to his house, and through the window we could see the fireplace blazing inside. It looked very inviting. We walked up his path to his door and rang the doorbell. When the door swung open, the captain appeared before us, smiling from ear to ear.

"Well, who do we have here? You two are a long way from the big city, aren't you?"

I shrugged playfully. "We just happened to be in the neighbourhood and thought we'd drop by to say hello."

"Not many in the neighbourhood this time of year unless they have hooves," he said, laughing. "Come on in out of the cold and warm up."

We stepped inside and found that it was even more inviting than it had looked from the outside. The fireplace was in full flame, warming us immediately as we took off our jackets.

"You just missed my better half," he said. "She went out snowshoeing. It's pretty quiet this time of year, so it's great for winter hikes and getting out on the snowshoes."

"Maybe she just needed to get out and have a break from your stories," I said with a grin.

"That *is* probably closer to the truth," he admitted. "How are you doing, Dawn? Is this your first time to Waterton Park?"

"I'm doing great, and I love it here!" she answered. "This is my first time, and I'm in awe. It's like going back in time with all the animals walking around town. You must love it up here."

"It's paradise," the captain stated simply. "I'm a lucky man, for sure."

Once we'd settled onto various easy chairs near the fire, he leaned back and stretched out his legs, crossing them at the ankles, and gave us a considering look. "So there must have been a reason for this trip. I know this place is a little off the beaten path, as nice as it is. So ... what brings you by?"

Dawn smiled affectionately at him. "We thought we'd come by to give you a gift. A little thank you for all the help you gave us. Mark?"

She turned to me and nodded, so I grabbed the bag that I'd tucked beside my chair and pulled it forward. "Well," I said, "since you *are* the captain, we thought we'd offer a gift with a nautical theme. Before you open it, though, I'd like to say a few words, if I could. First off, we truly want to thank you for spending time with us, first on the boat and then with both of us at our office. You went out of your way, and we really appreciate it."

The captain seemed a bit taken aback by all the fuss but pleased just the same. "You are both very welcome."

I handed him his gift. "Before you open it, you should know that this gift is symbolic of time, symbolic in two separate ways: First, it's for the time you gave us—time that took you away from your normal life, choosing to spend it with us instead—and we will be eternally grateful for that. And second, it symbolizes the new appreciation and friendship that Dawn and I now *have* with time.

You gave us some incredible insight that has already allowed us to have a certain hard conversation we needed to have. You taught us to respect our business's time but also the time of our team members, now and going forward, which has already made a real difference in our business. The former team member that we were having problems with, I'm happy to report, has landed on her feet elsewhere. The time you gave us truly was a gift, and we'll always be grateful to you."

The captain seemed visibly moved, though he was trying to hide it, so I decided to let him off the hook. "Okay, enough of that. Why don't you open your gift?"

As he pulled away the wrapping, his eyes lit up. "Oh, my goodness ... I know what this is!" He shook his head a bit in disbelief. "A marine chronometer, for telling time on a ship." He ran his hand over its antique finish and then looked up at us. "It's beautiful. Thanks so much for this."

"We thought it might be the perfect gift for a captain who spends time out on the water. We want you to think of time whenever you see it, on the boat or off."

"I'm ... I'm touched," he said. "Truly. For both the gift and the fact that you would take the time to hand-deliver it to me."

Dawn moved toward him with her arms out, and he stood up to receive her hug. "We'd never be in the position we're at with the company and our team if it wasn't for you and your words of wisdom."

I stayed seated, happily watching their embrace. The captain winked at me over her shoulder. *Or is he blinking away a tear?* Before I could figure it out, he pulled away from her and turned away, settling back into his chair.

"Well, thank you both very much. But now I've got to ask: How are things actually going with the business?"

Dawn and I looked at each other and then smiled as we turned back to the captain. I nodded toward her, signalling that she should bring him up to speed.

"You almost wouldn't believe it." She was beaming. "Our office is almost unrecognizable now in terms of the way it operates. And all credit for this transformation goes to you and the concepts you took us through."

"Lots of positive changes then." He nodded. "I won't take all that credit, though. I just gave you some ideas. You're the ones who must have taken those and put them into effect."

"Well," I said, "we couldn't have done it without you either way. After you saw us last, we decided to embrace the concepts you outlined, both in our roles and throughout the business. It took a bit of getting used to, actually living the CEO and COO roles, I must admit. But we decided to dive right into them, and your other suggestions as well. Positive things started to happen, and we have not looked back. The team is firing on all cylinders and has a clear vision of what the company is all about. We never could have gotten to this point without your guidance."

He shrugged modestly. "You just needed a little direction. You had all the tools within yourselves. Still ... I am so happy for you both, and for your business and your team."

As he admired his gift once again, I thought I could see his eyes shining a bit more than normal in the firelight. After a moment, he shook his head a bit and, blinking rapidly, he carefully set the gift down on a nearby side table, as if though it were truly precious to him. I wasn't sure who was more moved by all of this: him or me.

"So," he said then, as if to break the seriousness of the moment, "I hope you have time for a hot chocolate by the fire before you go. I have marshmallows!"

Laughing at that, I looked over at Dawn. "What do you think, COO?"

"It's up to you, CEO," she answered, snickering. "You're responsible for the vision of what we do, after all. I'm just the executioner. Do you envision us sitting by the fire with a hot chocolate in the near future?"

"I *can* see it, in fact." I smiled at them both. "I really can."

VISION MEETS EXECUTION
ADDITIONAL THOUGHTS

I have worked with countless businesses across the country, helping them to incorporate this "Vision meets Execution" approach into their business models. From hands-on experience, I have gained some interesting insight into the mindsets of business owners and leaders when they are first introduced to this approach. This is quite a new concept or approach, so most business owners have no reference point. They have not been taught this approach historically, nor have they seen it in action when they look to their peer group. This represents unchartered waters for them. The terms CEO and COO are not new to any of them, by any means, but the first hurdle they need to get over is the use of these terms every day within their business. It is not common practice to use these terms in any business with fewer than fifty people, so you can appreciate why a smaller business has a big adjustment to make in adopting these terms. These C-Suite terms are generally synonymous with big business.

At first, when this approach is introduced, the business owners seem to wrestle with these terms as though they're trying on a new outfit. They're not sure it fits. It's only with enough time do they get comfortable and discover that this outfit is perhaps their favourite. With even more time and training, they decide that it's the only outfit to wear. It is during this acclimatization process that I would typically start to see changes in the demeanour of the business owner, and they start to live the role. When I say, "live the role," I mean looking through the business's eyes as opposed to their own in every aspect of their lives. The leaders must be comfortable with putting down their old identity and picking up the identity of the business.

To arrive at this critical mindset, the leaders must put down the importance of status, or perceived status, that comes with the title of the role. Leaders often believe there is status associated with this role or title, and this flawed mindset is often their starting point. This needs to be adjusted in order to understand that only the results of the business matter, not any prestige or perceived prestige of the role. The viewpoint and acceptance that their business now comes first, in terms of their accountability and decision making (versus their historical approach of putting themselves before the business), is a big shift in mindset. Once they start to believe in this approach, they start to live the "results before status" mindset. It's quite a journey to get some leaders to this point, and it's not a journey for the faint of heart because it takes time and work.

The reward for the effort is a metamorphous that is amazing to watch from the outside. I would be remiss not to state that during this transformation stage, these CEOs often relapse to their former selves. Luckily for the business, the frequency and severity of these occurrences diminish over time. I chuckle when I think about some of the meetings I've had with these business owners over the years. Often these CEOs in the making would be caught between the various hats they'd been wearing, and I could see their struggles right before my eyes. Many times during our meetings I could see they were drifting back toward their former approaches, and the CEO within them would disappear right before my eyes. When this happened, I would stop the meeting and have to politely ask them to leave the meeting room with very specific instructions. They were to step outside and then send the CEO back in. The message was sent and quickly received. This was all part of the transformation process.

The second insight I've gained by being part of this "Vision meets Execution" process is that once the CEO and COO have arrived at the appropriate mindset, they can easily recognize the leadership of companies that *don't* follow this approach. I suspect it's much like a smoker who quits smoking; they are forever more conscious of the smell of smoke and are hypersensitive to this aroma. Many times, the CEO and I would discuss this phenomenon, and they'd point out to me how they could now see what other companies are still missing. This is a very satisfying discussion for me. I feel like a proud dad watching their children mature and demonstrate that they have the tools to take on the world. I'm sure most of you know that feeling. It's only when they fully arrive at this point in the process that I am confident their businesses will be successful for years to come.

The imagery that comes to mind for me on this transformation is from the old show from the early 1970s, *Kung Fu*. Master Po (an old wise Shaolin monk) challenges Kwai Chang Caine (a young monk referred to by Master Po as "Grasshopper") to snatch a pebble from his hand. If Grasshopper can get the pebble out of Master Po's hand before he closes it, that would indicate that it was time for Grasshopper to leave the monastery, as he would have learned everything he needed to learn to take on the world. When I look back over the years of working with all the CEO and COOs I have encountered, I am proud to say that a lot of pebbles have been successfully snatched from my hand. Proud moments indeed.

Through reading this book and putting it into action within your business, let's see if you can wake up one day with the pebble in *your* hand. It is now time to take the concepts, approaches, and ideas that were laid out in this story from the abstract to the concrete and into the business world in which you operate. Too often, we fail to put into play the ideas we come across, whether sourced from a book you read or just from the people you meet in your life and share ideas with. Why this lack of execution? Perhaps you are the only camel in your caravan and currently have too much straw on your back. Perhaps you have not built the support system you need. Perhaps you're reluctant to add anyone to your team, as you think this will be more of a headache than it is worth, so you have convinced yourself that your status quo is appropriate. Perhaps it is your mindset that is stopping you from taking that first step. In all these cases, *you* are the common denominator that acts as a barrier to the other side, between where you are and where you could be. There is only one thing to do: Take the first step. This will get the ball rolling, and your business will start moving forward.

If you find yourself hesitating to take the step forward, then you must first ask yourself two simple sets of questions:

1. Do you want a different outcome for your business? Is there a feeling inside of you that there must be more to business than you have experienced so far? Are you tired of where your business sits as compared to where you think it should sit? Do you think the pace of the business is slower than it should be? In your business, is there more work than hours in the day?

If you have answered yes to any of the questions in this initial set, then you have arrived at the door of the final question—and rather than a second set, there is really only one. This is the question you must ask yourself before unlocking the door to answers.

2. Are you open to going on a journey of understanding that will position you and your business in a better place? And I mean really open. Many people quickly answer "Yes" to this question, but deep down, they have not made the commitment to living that answer.

Look inside yourself to find your answer. If you are now truly committed and willing to take the steps, I have laid out the start of your path in the following pages, laying out the practical applications of the key points within the story you have just read, designed to make the actions you will want (and need) to take much easier. All that is required of you now is to take that first step. Your pebble awaits you.

CEO ATTRIBUTES

Although I am sure there are endless lists of what makes a CEO great, I have decided to focus on only four attributes. Through my years of practical experience, I have found that the four I have outlined in the story you have now read stand out as being of the highest priority list for guiding a company successfully. If you take the time to understand each of these four and use them properly every day, they will provide an excellent foundation for success in the CEO role and in your business.

First CEO Attribute: TRUST

SpongeBob: "What if I break your
trust someday?"
Patrick: "Trusting you is *my decision*, proving me
wrong is *your choice*."

Do you trust your team members, and more importantly, do you trust yourself enough to empower them? Often when I am dealing with the CEO and their surrounding team, a common pattern emerges. There seems to be a reluctance by the CEO to allow anyone to get full autonomy over their roles, and to trust the COO with any part of decision making. These CEOs are quick to give a title to a person within the organization but very slow to give the much-needed autonomy of that role. Plainly put, they want to ensure that they are the decision makers in every instance. This pattern can also be seen within the COOs of the company. We need "autonomy of role" throughout the organization. The question I pose to you is this: Which approach are you currently taking in your leadership? Full autonomy of decision making for the COO and other roles within the team, or full control of every decision by you or someone else on the team? Maybe somewhere in between? We need to journey toward trusting the COO and the people on our team and allowing the autonomy of the roles within your company. I want you to take the time to rate yourself on the following questions from one to ten (with ten being the best or highest):

1. Do you, the CEO, allow the COO on your team autonomy within their role?

2. If the COO was asked the same question of the CEO, what would their rating be on them?

3. Does the COO allow members of their team autonomy in their roles?

4. If the team members were asked the same question of the COO, what would their rating of them be?

5. Do you, the CEO, or your COO, allow each other to get away with not releasing the parts of your roles that should not be in your lane?

If we scored low on any of the answers from the above questions, then we need to ask ourselves one more question: Why the reluctance to allow others to have the autonomy of the decision? Although there are countless books, articles, and studies on micromanagement and its negative impact on teams and businesses, this approach seems to still be more alive than ever and prevalent in the leadership of businesses today. The command-and-control approach many leaders take will limit the effectiveness of any organization in terms of their desired pace, scale, and outcome. Not only does it hurt the organization in terms of outcomes but also has a detrimental impact on the development of the team within the company. When leaders must have every decision run through their fingers, they don't realize that this is actually not leadership but management. Leaders, on the other hand, train those in their organization to understand the problem and then solve it. Vastly different approaches.

The CEO should empower the COO, and the COO should empower all other team members, to be the decision makers within their individual roles. In business and in life what we should do and what we actually do can be worlds apart. There is often a struggle within our minds in terms of allowing ourselves to let go of the steering wheel and allow others to drive. We seem to want to keep the pebbles of learning to ourselves. We have a hard time seeing what our CEO or COO role would be if we empowered others and just let go. How did we arrive at this place of resistance, and what is stopping us from embracing this freeing approach? The answer could be in our exposure to experiences that have taught us or shaped us to believe this is the way to deal with team members. Never trust anyone to do a better job or give up control of a situation might be our mantra. We might believe that this is the way to handle team members because this is what we have witnessed in our work lives, and this seems like the logical way to handle things. Regardless of what thought process steered us to where we sit today, it is time for a different approach. Although it might feel counterintuitive it is time to trust the process of autonomy. If you trust the process and allow others to control the decision making of their roles, it's a very freeing experience. This letting go allows us to discover a universal law of business, which is that our primary role as leaders within a company is to get out of the way when it comes to decision making and allow others to flourish. The reward for this new approach is very liberating. We can use the time saved from micromanaging people to do our own roles even better. This new approach will add increased value to our business.

After this self-examination, having now rated ourselves and the people in our organization, if we discover that our scores are low, then it is time for action. We need to know what steps to take to start putting this "trust" environment into play within your business. Here are some steps and ideas to consider:

1. Start the process. CEOs, allow your COO to start taking on the autonomy of their role and the decision-making process. COOs, allow your team to start taking on the autonomy of their roles and the decision-making process. As a reminder, this is a not a short process and will need time to develop to its fullest potential. There will be times when you want to jump right in and revert to old ways, especially when things don't go the way you thought they would. Resist. Allow time for this process to take hold.

2. Don't throw your COO or team members to the wolves. To embrace this trust and "autonomy of decision" approach doesn't mean you give a task or project to someone and never get involved again. This might feel counterintuitive to what should happen, but when it comes to support, it is not an all or nothing approach. You still need to show support for the COO and team members so that they can become better at doing this as well. The key is not to jump back in and take the ball out of their hands. Be more like a coach on the sideline and let them learn to throw the football.

VISION MEETS EXECUTION

3. Ensure that communication and clarity are at the foundation of this learning. This involves making sure that all parties, the CEO, COO and the team members, understand the expectations of their role. Between all parties, you need to have an open communication that goes both ways without judgement. Show support instead of judgement. This is a great spot to work on two-way candour between CEO and COO, and COO and any team member.

4. Understand that mistakes will happen, and don't abandon the game plan at the first sign of a mistake. These are just the growing pains. There *will* be small missteps in trying to put this overall approach into action. Always remember the small mistakes that can arise during this process and their overall cost to the business will pale when compared to the larger mistake of not allowing the decision making to flow properly through the organization. The longer we hold on to the autonomy rather than pass it on, the higher the cost will be to the organization.

Be the positive change in your business.

Second CEO Attribute: DECISION VS. OUTCOME

"You can't make decisions based on fear and the
possibility of what might happen."
—Michelle Obama

The CEO role is one where decision making is front and centre. Within this role, there is no place to hide. Decisions need to be made and will be transparent for all to see. Welcome to leadership. We need not fear this part of the role. Instead, we need to embrace this fact because it represents what many would consider to be the best part of the role. We must start to create a mindset where we don't fear the decisions that we have to make. We need to be at peace with the fact that decision making is just part and parcel of the role of any leader. Too often, leaders are letting this fear, along with a host of other factors (such as anxiety, public opinions, and stress), shape and steer their decision-making approach. To compound this issue and make it even tougher, the role today has another factor to contend with: social media.

We live in an age where everything is highly visible, and everyone has more access to information, or at least parts of it. This is especially true in terms of the outcomes of our decisions. Once the world sees the outcome of a decision, they become armchair experts and weigh in with everything they think was wrong with it. With the outcome already firmly in their hands, they become experts on what *should* have happened. Unfortunately, having the outcome ahead of time is not a luxury afforded to any CEO or any leader in their decision-making process. The CEO or leaders must decide on a path while the outcome is still unknown. As such, we must be careful when we use outcomes to conclude whether our decisions are right or wrong. The decision and the outcome are actually independent of one another and should be viewed accordingly.

How do we start to really separate the outcome from the decision in terms of our approach? Given all the factors that can go into a decision, which seem endless given the data-filled world we live in today, it is imperative that leaders know when to say stop to the stream of information to consider and just make the final decision. Otherwise, you risk the adage of paralysis by analysis, where you don't decide because of the sheer volume of information and fear of the outcome. You need to find the balance of what's too little information and what is too much. This sweet spot is where you want to be. But how do you arrive at this decision-making mecca where everything is in balance?

You need to gather the information from all sources, both formally and informally, to increase your awareness of the impact of the decision on all stakeholders. You will need to know where the team will stand on this decision. You should have the self-awareness and social awareness of the impact of the decision you're considering, using your emotional intelligence (EQ) along with your IQ in the decision-making process. Once all these factors, along with any others you need to add to the process, are considered, then it is time to make the decision. The outcome will arrive at your doorstep not long after.

There is no doubt that once we see the outcome of any decision, this can help us gain insight into the decision-making process. Once we have the outcome, we need to take steps to re-examine the decision-making process in its entirety, looking for any flaws in the process. Within the examination of a past decision, we want to look at the various components of the decision. We do this to see if we could have improved on the information we had, or its sources, the inputs we used, and the overall process. When looking back at a decision-making process, we need to examine the process for any flaws in the approach. Fully understanding this examination could be completed in minutes, or maybe an hour or two.

This is not about spending weeks examining every detail of every component of the decision. The sort of examination I'm talking about is just a quick mental run through of it, so that you are at peace with the process. Start with this question to yourself: Was the process I used to come to the decision sound? If the answer to this question is yes, it is time to move on. If the answer to the question is no, then you need to figure out what needs to be changed or worked on to make it a better process. Identify the needed change, fix it, and then move on. Anytime we get an outcome from a decision, repeat this self-assessment process of the decision. Too often I see people drifting backwards in history and punishing themselves for some unfortunate outcome, telling themselves, "I should have," "I wish I would have," or "I *knew* it!" Doing this serves no purpose to ourselves. These phrases should be eliminated from your vocabulary. Too often people in business, and in life, spend too much time and energy in the pursuit of a time machine with which they could go back and change something that would have improved an outcome. This is a great premise for a Netflix series but an absolute waste of time in our real lives.

One of the clearest examples of "decision making versus outcome" (outside the business world) can be found in the main event of the World Series of Poker. This is a championship no-limit game of Texas Hold 'em poker that is held every year in Las Vegas. It's a simple game at first glance, with each person getting two playing cards from a standard deck of cards, which they keep hidden from the other players. The rest of the cards needed to determine a winner are community cards that are shared and visible to everyone at the table. In this winner-take-all tournament, with each hand dealt, players must make decisions that will help them to stay alive or get eliminated.

Each person must weigh factors like their chip count, tournament position, table position, historical play of their opponents, and so on into their decision-making process every step along the way. This decision-making process is usually completed in less than a minute and is repeated thousands of times during the tournament. At some point, a player's entire stack of poker chips will be in the middle of the table, and their tournament life will be on the line—all based on a decision they have made given the information of the moment. The outcome is out of their hands at that point and is independent of the decision they have made. All that is left to see is if they win the hand and get to play on or lose it and are eliminated from the tournament. It is after this outcome, when a player loses, that you really see that person's decision-making process.

If they know that they have weighed the factors logically and made an informed decision based on the information they had, they will be at peace regardless of any outcome, able to just

run the examination process back through their minds and move on. Their decision-making process was sound, and the outcome was independent of the decision. On the other hand, those players who do not have a sound decision making process and who go on instinct or try to short cut the decision-making process and just go all in because they feel lucky in that moment will invariably struggle with their decision and agonize over it for hours, days, or even years after the tournament. It will haunt them, and all because they were betting on the *outcome* instead of on the actual process of coming to a sound decision.

Don't let the outcome of *any* decision rent space in your head beyond using it for a simple re-examination of your decision-making process so that you can improve it going forward.

What questions would I ask myself if I was trying to put this examination process into play for a decision with an unfortunate outcome? Here is list to get you started:

1. Were there outside factors that impaired your decision-making process, which you don't want to impair it in the future:

   Examples of outside factors could include the following: *political influence* (Was there a person or group of people who influenced the decision in some way it should not have?); fear (some perceived consequence of the decision, like losing your position or the respect of the team); the *desire* to keep everything status quo.

   It is imperative that our decision-making process is pristine in terms of negative outside influence.

2. Were all the sources of information current and reliable?

   Decisions are only as good as the information we receive. We need to examine if all our sources are as good as they can be. Are all the sources giving accurate information? Based upon the quality of the source of information, can we rely on them for future decisions?

3. Are you using your past experiences in the right context and application?

   Experience gained from the past can be valuable to you ... until it is not. We want to take the lessons of the past and bring them forward, but we want to do it cautiously. We must understand that conditions and situations change with time, such as the people on the team, the overall work environment (both with the country you're working in and the workplace itself), and finally the dynamics of the work environment.

   Make sure you are factoring these ever-changing variables into your decision-making approach going forward.

4. Did you factor EQ (emotion quotient) and IQ into your decision appropriately?

   This question and its answer allow us to see if we are considering all factors in making our decisions. Often CEOs make decisions but are missing the impact of the team and the people on this process. This will become apparent once a decision is announced or the outcome is available. We cannot make decisions in isolation, unaware or uncaring of how it impacts the organization on at all levels. People matter. Ensure that you use all the tools available to you in your decision-making process.

5. If in the exact situation again, not knowing the outcome in advance, would you make the same decision?

   The answer to this question is very important. If your *first* instinct is to answer "No" to this question, you might be factoring in the outcome too much. If you see decisions through the outcome lens, you need to work on separating outcome from your decision-making process. We should not be looking at the outcome as determining the quality of the decision. If we did, we would change every decision we made that ended poorly. We just need to be able to assure ourselves that, if we had the same information and process today, we would make the same decision, regardless.

If you *would* make the same decision, then you can be sure that your decision-making process is correct. It is hard not to want to be sure of the outcome before deciding, but we are rarely, if ever, afforded that luxury. Always continue to improve your decision-making process so that your outcomes also improve over time.

As a CEO, when you execute the decision-making process well, it can really inspire the team. This instills confidence in your team and heightens the trust of the entire team. Even when the outcome is negative, those CEOs who take fully accountability for their process set an example to the team that helps rally their conviction to the firm and one another. Remember that the team *wants* you to lead them and help them grow professionally. They don't want you to be perfect. They want you to be human. The team members can only grow if the company is growing as well ... with a sound decision-making approach.

Third CEO Attribute: SHADOW CASTING

*"Your business will only get as big as
the shadow of your character."*
– Orrin Woodward

A lot of responsibility comes with the role of CEO. The primary responsibility, which some leaders fear and struggle with the most, is that you are the example for the business in terms of conduct and behaviour. The entire team looks to you and your actions as a guideline for them to follow. This can be overwhelming for some leaders, as they feel they have the eyes of the world on them. They are always in the spotlight, which means they are judged more on their actions than their words. Our actions will guide the team in terms of the conduct that is truly allowed within the walls of the business. We need to understand this key point, as a CEO's poor example is what leads too many businesses to have poor cultures. Leaders need to lead by example.

Many leaders think this spotlight on our actions shuts off when the workday is done, at which time they feel that can become a different person. In their minds, once they leave work, all bets are off and poor behaviour can be allowed to happen. Unfortunately, this is where most leaders fail, not understanding that the consistency of our behaviour has no time schedule. We need to strive to be the same person in all aspects of our lives to give the business, and its team members, the best chance to see a great example of leadership.

The spotlight of the role should not be a concern for those who are consistent both in and outside work. But what if you find the spotlight concerning, worried that it might shine its light onto some behaviour set that you are not proud of or want to change.

If you find yourself in this situation, how do you go about making the desired changes to your behaviour in order to be at peace with the spotlight? There are several steps you can take to become more consistent in your behaviour and become the leader you want to be.

Step 1. Get accurate data or feedback on your behaviour.

The first thing you would want to understand is which behaviours are casting negative shadows on your business or its team members. I believe most of us know when our behaviour is out of line, but there are instances where people are not self-aware enough to see themselves and how their behaviours can cause issues. To take the steps forward to improve any behaviour set, we must know where we are at in terms of other people's perception. The goal would be to find the most accurate feedback you can for your starting point of self-improvement. The higher the quality of the feedback, the easier it is to understand where you're at and where you need to go to accomplish your desired outcome.

The good news is that your team has the information you're looking for. The bad news is that getting this information might be harder than you think. Getting the most accurate feedback from any of your team members could be a challenge depending upon the type of environment you've created historically within the business. Anyone you approach and attempt to ask for this candid type of feedback on yourself would have to trust that they are safe in delivering this type of feedback to you and will not face any negative consequence for their honesty. If the safety and trust aren't there, then you will get watered down answers that are not reflective of what they are truly thinking. These courtesy answers will add little value and will not steer you where you need to go for self-improvement.

How do you know what type of environment you have created within your business? A simple answer is to ask yourself whether or not you have been getting regular feedback from the team on your conduct, or any feedback at all. This answer will give you some insight into the true nature of the communication and relationship you have with team members. It's very likely that you don't have the type of open communication and relationship you would need to get the candid answers you desire. You might wonder why I would come to that conclusion, but it is rooted in the fact that if you had an open communication, you would likely already know what you need to know. This is the ironic part of the whole process. If you had a healthy, open communication environment, then you would already know what behaviours you need to address and be working on them.

If you find yourself in a business and culture where this has not been established, then my suggestion would be to go to the most trusted person you have within the team. If you have a COO in your life, then this would be a great starting point. Explain what you are trying to accomplish and ask for their honest feedback. You will have to likely promise that this won't impact this person's job or everyday work situation in order to get a higher degree of candour. This source could be the best starting source as you work on having open communication between the two of you.

If there is still a reluctance from your COO or the team to provide the information you seek, then you might have to get an independent party from outside the business. This third party can take steps to have discussions with the team to try to ascertain the needed information as well as some context around referenced situations. The only thing to consider is that the team would have to feel safe in providing this information and would likely provide more honest feedback to this third party than to you yourself. Once you receive some feedback from any source, you have a great starting point.

Step 2. Accept the data to be true.

This is an area that needs the most attention. In my experience, most leaders have a type-A personality and don't want to hear about their shortcomings. In their minds, it is especially humbling to have someone else point them out. This is often because they are highly intelligent and feel that they are smarter than the other team members, failing to realize that it is likely their EQ score that is causing them to not see the truth of any situation, not their IQ. Put your pride aside if you really want to take steps to allow both your company and yourself to be the best they can be. You must be willing and open to accepting the feedback from individuals on your team, regardless of their role. Often upon hearing such feedback, the CEO will struggle to accept it as factual or accurate. It's usually not just accepted at face value, or else it is rationalized, or in some cases, rejected completely. Learn to accept feedback at face value or search yourself to discover *why* you can't accept it at face value. You need to look within yourself to accept it as the truth. If you can do this, then you are well on your way to the next step in the process.

Step 3. Plan your steps for action

Now that you have accurate data and have accepted it, what should you do next? It is time to put into action a plan to make the accuracy of this feedback a thing of the past. This is a great opportunity to tackle two key areas during this plan stage. The first area, which is rather obvious, is that it is addressing any shortcomings or behaviour sets that need improvement. A big win for your personal development. The second area that will get addressed during this plan-execution stage is that you will start to strengthen the open communication style that is needed for the business and each leader within it. Establishing open communication as part of your process going forward will build in a design that helps you to improve on any shortcomings you discover about yourself as part of the ongoing feedback.

Once you have the feedback, it is time to determine the support needed to address it. You need to look at the feedback and determine if you need outside help to correct this issue or if it is something you can correct yourself. Depending on the depth of the issue, you might need to get outside help to address whatever is at the root of the feedback issues. If it is a deeper issue than you can remedy on your own, then it's time to look to outside resources. These resources could range from counselling to peer-group support. Always start with outside support, if needed, and then work your way back into the team. If it is an issue that you feel you can tackle, then look for support within your team.

While you are working on the behaviour change, find an accountability partner. You can do this by asking the COO or any team member to help you stay accountable to the changes you are trying to achieve. Allow them to point out when this behaviour pattern is occurring and then take steps to have these occurrences dimmish over time. Again, it is important never to punish your accountability partner, as they are just trying to support the change *you* are trying to make.

If feedback worked to unveil a behaviour concern, then ensure that you continue the feedback loop as part of the process. It is important to keep establishing a feedback loop in which the team gives you the much-desired feedback so you can continue the journey of self-improvement. It is not a one-and-done situation. All of us should be in a constant improvement mode, trying to be a better version of ourselves every day. An ongoing feedback loop within the business will help ensure that poor behaviour and setbacks are caught early and addressed early. Become the leader you are destined to be.

Fourth CEO Attribute: CANDOUR

*"When two people always agree,
one of them is unnecessary."*
—William Wrigley Jr.

I believe that candour is a lost skill that most leaders today are missing. The reason I use the term "lost" is that it used to be more common, but somewhere along the way, we seem to have lost the ability to have open, frank discussions with one another. Part of the blame might be that it is not a skill at the forefront of many teachings. Off the top of my head, I cannot recall a business course called "Candour 101," yet it is incredibly important to the successful operations of a business in terms of team communication. If the business does not have candour at the root of its communication, it robs the team members of an opportunity to learn and grow. Candour needs to be part of the day-to-day functionality of any business. We often think of candour within a business not by its usage but rather by its absence. Its absence appears in three distinct areas within a business.

The first is in leadership. Leaders need to communicate their expectations of each person's role within a business. This will give each team member the best chance to be clear on what they need to focus on in terms of their role. That requires feedback, with candour at its root. It serves no purpose to explain anything but your true perception or feelings of the role someone is doing. We think politeness or diplomacy protects them, but it doesn't. It actually harms them. Proper constructive feedback on a regular basis allows people to learn and grow to become a better version of themselves. This type of feedback can be both informal in nature, such as quick chats or friendly visits, or it can be formal in nature, such as quarterly performance reviews or conversations. Both are designed to be a mechanism for feedback.

The second area where candour is noticeably absent is when a leader wants feedback from his team. This type of 360-degree feedback helps the leaders get information that is invaluable to them. As referenced in the previous section, this information can help them in terms of their effectiveness and behaviours as a leader. It also can be a great source of information for decision making. The more accurate the data, the better the decisions that are based on it. Too often, because we have not created an environment that is conducive to an open, honest, candid approach, we get only information that is superficial in nature, watered-down information that serves little purpose for the advancement of the team members or the business.

The final area where candour is noticeably absent is in the "group think" area. This leads to teams adopting a herd mentality, with no one daring to think differently or risk being ostracized from the group. We all have seen movies or TV shows where a company is full of "yes" men. These are people who agree with everything a leader says. Too often, we get groups of people who forget that the core of any group is its individuals, so instead, they always agree with the group consensus. Their individuality is lost. We need people to express their views so that the group can strengthen and improve, with everyone adding new perspectives and insight. Consensus takes that opportunity away and weakens the group. We don't need to disagree just for the sake of disagreeing, but we need a healthy variety of opinions to see the best path forward for everyone.

If you decide that it's time to put candour to use within your business model, you must take it slow. You need to ease your way into the pool. Often people will dive in headfirst and just say, "I am going to be candid going forward." Can you say "culture shock?" The problem with this all-or-nothing approach is that we have already conditioned everyone around us for a certain environment. Most businesses don't have an open, candid environment or culture. If you start out at 100 percent, to them it's like getting hit by a tidal wave. It is imperative that we ease our way into this process so as not to lose the team during the process. The business leaders can start to put small steps into play, giving people time to get used to this approach.

It starts with explaining to the entire team what you mean by "candour" and why it is important for the business to develop a more candid environment. You could further offer examples of candour and how all team members would ideally deliver and receive it. You could challenge the team to slowly start using it in their conversations with their fellow team members. Of course, you would need to ensure that the team understands that candour is about the *other* person, sharing information honestly for *their* benefit rather than their own. Another important step is ensuring that candidness does not get punished but rather rewarded within the organization. We need to slowly integrate this approach until it is part of the DNA of the business, driven by the acceptance of the team members.

To help the team understand the culture you want them to strive for in the future, we need to paint a visual of what it would look like and how we would stage our way to this future state. A visual of a more open and candid environment, over time, to help the business function better as a whole. This visual would be done in stages so that everyone is comfortable with each step before moving to the next. Using a survey as an example, you could stage this so that team members get used to the idea of sharing feedback. Stage one could be an anonymous survey to get open feedback from all team members. Explain to them that, eventually, when they are ready for stage two, the business will arrive at a place where everyone would be adding their names to the feedback survey. Once that becomes normal and accepted, you hope to reach stage three, where no survey is required and every on the team can simply communicate what is on their minds in an open, candid culture.

A team that arrives at a point where candid discussion are now the norm will be a healthier organization than one that doesn't have this as the root of their communication. Candour needs to be the main building block for the strong foundation of any successful business.

First COO Attribute: *TEAM UTILIZATION*

"If you delegate tasks, you create followers; if you delegate authority, you create leaders."
—Craig Groeschel

The COO's role within the business is key to the execution of everything that needs to be done in order to assure the success of the business. This role requires a person to keep their finger on the pulse of all team members and their ability to work as a cohesive unit that creates executional output. One of the key areas that needs to be focused on by the COO is the workload distribution within the business, identifying where the bottlenecks of workflow are occurring. We must guard against bottlenecks of workflow, where one or more team members become the roadblocks to an even distribution of the workload.

All team members within an organization, including the CEO and COO, have been known to participate in this counterproductive behaviour of roadblocking. Whether they realize it or not, they can become barriers to the success of the business. Why would the key team members create barriers to the business? There could be several reasons for this, from the perspective of a team member:

1. Control. A person might feel threatened by the idea of giving a responsibility, project, or task away, worried that they simply can do it better than themselves, or maybe even that the person they share it with might outshine them or encroach on their territory. In all these cases, the potential sharing of their workload is seen as a threat rather than an opportunity for the organization to function better. In these instances, we put our own needs and fears ahead of the

team and its functionality. This approach is very punitive to the team instead of being beneficial to it.

2. <u>Doubt of skill set</u>. Often people don't believe the person to whom they will have to assign a task is skilled enough to handle it. Whether this is factual or not, it is accurate in the mind of the person who will not release the work. They don't realize that if they don't pass along the work, we can never come to an accurate conclusion of where the problem lies. We need to give the person a chance to develop their skill set in order to become skilled. Alternatively, we need to recognize that they are not capable of handling the role they are in. Both outcomes provide clarity to the organization.

3. <u>Trust or respect is not there.</u> Often people do not trust or respect the person to whom they need to pass the work. Maybe they think they do not share the same work ethics, integrity, or commitment to the business. This could be from actual experiences with the person or from second-hand information, or this could be fabricated in their own mind. In any case, this poses a problem to the flow of work until it is resolved.

4. <u>Assuming they are qualified by role title.</u> We always assume that everyone has a vast amount of experience in the work world or that they should pick things up easily if they have a certain role. Often the reason they become the barrier is simply that they do not understand. Don't assume a person always knows how to do something based on their role or experience. Even if they have years of experience, it doesn't mean these years were ones that involved learning the right

way to execute a role. Take some time to ensure the person you are trying to work with understands what is being asked of them and are open to saying that they don't understand or know the best way to tackle something.

Whatever the reasons for the roadblocks, it plays itself out consistently in terms of the pattern of thoughts. We overwork ourselves by not allowing anyone to handle any part of the project or task. We say to ourselves it is "just easier if I do it" or "it won't take long, so I'll just quickly do it." By retaining all parts of a project or task, we feel that we don't have to worry about someone else's contribution. This type of behaviour by a team member within an organization will put undue risk on both the person and the business. It is a risk to the person because it is a recipe for burnout. The risk for the business rises as the knowledge of a business becomes proprietary to a person rather than the business. We need to allow others to share in lifting the load to protect both team members and the business in the long run.

What if a situation arises where the person who is hoarding the workload must ask others for help? If they find themselves in a situation where they need to, or are forced to, give any part of the task away, they do so reluctantly and still want to monitor every step that is involved with the other person's involvement. They decide at this point it is better to continually "look over the shoulder" of the person assigned this task. This has two obvious problems. The first is that it is a highly inefficient use of the time of the person assigning the task. They are, in fact, still doing the task as defined by the amount of time it is renting in their heads. The second problem is that we don't allow others to learn to bring up their skill set and become the trusted, reliable person we want them to be. The idea of involving others is easy to understand on the surface but harder to make a reality for those who want to do it all. We often revert back to the micromanage approach, where we pass work along and then check on the status. If we find the person has not completed the work, and we determine they are too busy, we cannot let ourselves say the famous words: "Oh, you're busy ... I will take that back." We often do not allow for the system to clear itself of the bottlenecks because we *are* the bottlenecks. The bottlenecks need to disappear if we want sustainable and growing output. When we feel we need to control every situation, it makes for a barrier that slows down a business's effectiveness and pace of execution.

If these roadblocks are popping up within the business, you need to start to work with the people who are the architects of them. This could very well include the CEO or the COO, which you would think should be the last people on this list. Whoever is on the list needs to take steps to remove themselves from it so that a business has no one on this list. We can do this by putting into play this four-step process to try to bring the person along.

A. Clearly outline the pattern to the person. Most likely they will be aware of it, but this way you have a solid starting point. Try to dive into the reasons they feel this approach is happening in the first place. Work to understand where they are coming from in terms of the reason.

B. Outline together the steps you will take to improve this behaviour. This could be creating or strengthening a feed-back loop so they can feel things are being handled. Clear accountability on all parties helps things function better. It could be working on trust between people and within the organization itself. It could be outlining clarity of the role and expectations so that everyone knows what is needed and expected.

C. Monitor the progress. You need to create a process where you are giving constant feedback on how the process is going. This will allow all team members a clear understanding of the progress in these areas.

D. Decide what actions need to be taken if no progress comes. This is easier if we are talking about the COO dealing with some team member other than the CEO. What if the CEO does not or will not change? Then it is decision time for the COO, fully understanding that the likelihood of the CEO changing, at this point, would be diminishing. But what if you looked in the mirror as the COO and discovered it was you who was the roadblock? Now you would know what should be running through your CEO's mind. It is possibly decision time for them. It is important to have open, candid conversations throughout this process so that you can understand where all parties sit in terms of their mindset.

By the COO overseeing an organizational process whereby we clearly define each role and job description and ensure that each team member is staying true to this process, we create an environment of success. This clear, candid, and repeatable process is key for the wellbeing of the company. This will allow for optimization of the workload and the best development of each team member, and ensures that everyone on the team, with no exceptions, is contributing to the overall success of the business.

Second COO Attribute: THREE Ps

*"You don't build a business, you build people, then
people build business."*
—**Zig Ziglar**

Every business should know that people are the key to its success. However, businesses also know that people, and managing people specifically, come with challenges at times. Challenges like how to get the team members to understand their roles and support each other in their roles so that everyone within the walls can be successful. How do you go about getting the team members to communicate better to one another and be aligned to what the business needs? The people side of the business is perhaps the most difficult area to deal with. When you get people, each with unique personalities and agendas, in close proximity to one another, problems will always arise. The COO needs to have a process to deal with these problems in a systematic way. Given the fact that these problems will appear on the plate of not only the COO but everyone in the organization, we need to have a simple and clear way to deal with them. The Three Ps and Three Cs process will help and is invaluable to handling people's problems. Let's break it down.

THREE P'S

PROBLEM	PROCESS	PERSON

It is imperative that we deal with identifying the problem first and then work our way across the page in order. "Problem" first, then "Process," and finally "Person."

Problem: These could also be called concerns, issues, or situations.

Process: What system or repeatable process do we have in place to handle the task or situation in which the problem occurred? This is the step-by-step, documented (whether written in hard copy or virtually) approach to handling this task. This should be clear and concise and easily teachable.

Person: This can be a team member, or it could be a business, entity, government, or institution. This "person" is whomever, or whatever, has the finger of blame pointed at them.

In everyday business (and life), problems arise where we think the problem is about a person. How we deal with them, and more importantly, the process we use, will determine our success in resolving the problem, as well as its likely recurrence. We want to create a repeatable way to deal with the problem and simultaneously create an opportunity for those involved to learn. By using this as a teaching opportunity, the likelihood of the same problems reoccurring diminishes. In business, these saved hours in the future allow for the company's greater efficiency and increased pace. When a problem arrives involving a person, we must not make the mistake of bypassing the process involved and just focussing on that person's portion of the problem. This is where most people make the error, and it causes lots of lost time for team members, and in turn, for the business.

Let's use an example: Someone approaches you, the COO, with a problem. Mr. Smith, a client, has phoned in and complained that his investment statement is way down and believes we don't know how to handle investments. His complaint feels inaccurate, as our firm is very process driven in their investment approach, so it doesn't seem possible that his investments are down in value. Susie, the team member who is responsible for the investment statements, must have dropped the ball. We obviously don't like clients thinking us incompetent as a business or as one that doesn't take the stewardship of their money seriously. Susie's effectiveness and professionalism is the COO's overall responsibility, although there is another person Susie reports to directly in between them. At first blush, we think Susie might be the problem. It is at this fork in the road where we either investigate the "process" or we jump right over to the "person," namely Susie. Both potential paths will have an impact on where our business goes in the long term. Jumping right to the person would be a critical error in terms of our approach. We know we need to choose the right path, so we step back and think about the Three Ps: problem, process, person, in that order. It is clear what the problem is, as defined by Mr. Smith's complaint. We know, or think we know, that it involves Susie. But what about the process, which is how it came about? Following the step-by-step approach of the Three Ps, we know cannot jump to the person until we have investigated the process involved in how this problem happened. It is at this point we need to draw a vertical line down the page to clearly separate the process from the person. Here is how this would look:

THREE P'S

PROBLEM	PROCESS	PERSON
Mr. Smith's Complaints		Susie

With some digging into the process of how investment account statements are dealt with, we discover that the computer program that manages the client-account statements Susie is responsible for sending out has recently been changed, no longer automatically consolidating the holdings on the statements to reflect an accurate picture of the overall holdings. On further investigation, we discover that this change had never been explained to Susie or the clients. If Susie had been informed and trained on the new process, she could have given the clients a heads up. Upon discovering this lapse in training and clarity, it becomes clear that none of the blame lies with Susie, and in fact, the entire problem, and Mr. Smith's complaint, is the business's fault.

We can see from the above example that if we had jumped to a conclusion that Susie was responsible, the outcome would have been problematic, unfair to Susie, and would have done nothing to keep the same problem from happening again. We can never fix our attention on the "person" until we have taken the time to fully understand the "process."

THREE P'S

PROBLEM	PROCESS	PERSON
Mr. Smith's Complaints	Old Process of using consolidated statements New Process of Using Third Party Statements Direct report properly coached on New Process Susie Coached on New Process	Susie
CLARITY	COACHING	CONDUCT

Let's change one thing and rerun this scenario. Imagine we were looking into the process and discovered that this new process had been clearly explained to the person who *oversees* Susie. At that point, we could potentially assume that Susie must have been trained by her immediate supervisor and so conclude that Susie is at fault. But again, we are at a fork in the road. Although the new process was explained to Susie's supervisor, we do not know if it was indeed filtered down to Susie. We cannot cross over the line that falls between the process and person until we run *another* set of rectangles and complete the Three Cs: "Clarity," "Coaching," and "Conduct."

Clarity. This box refers to "Clarity of Role" within the business. What is it you do? This is a clear job description that outlines required duties for success in the role.

Coaching. This refers to whether or not you have you been trained on all the components of your role. Has the firm adequately coached you on both the technical side and non-technical aspects of your role?

Conduct. This is the behaviour set with which you fulfil the role, with its coaching, to become successful. How do you act, behave, and conduct yourself within your role?

Before pausing to consider the three Cs, we were set to cross the line from the process to the person, but there was still some uncertainty. We still need to *answer* the three Cs before we get to Susie herself.

Clarity: Does Susie understand her role within the company? Have we provided a clear understanding of what is involved in her role and our expectations of her being successful?

Coaching: Have we taken the steps to coach and train Susie on all parts of her role, including any changes that might have been made? These would include technical training, ensuring that she is proficient at all her duties. Have we coached Susie on the non-technical side? The EQ/IQ (Emotional Quotient/Intelligence) aspects of her role?

These first two, "Clarity" and "Coaching," are 100 percent the responsibility of the business. Without exception. We have either done a good job on this or we haven't. Time to look in the mirror.

Conduct: What behaviour set has Susie decided to apply to her work life? How does she interact with others? Is she adding value to the company or taking value from the company? Susie is responsible for her own behaviour set. One hundred percent. No exceptions.

We need to go through each of the first two Cs in order, listing the things we have done in those areas, and grade ourselves on how we well we think we did.

Once we have graded ourselves in these first two areas, *our* responsibilities, the actions that follow should reflect those grades. If we have a failing grade in either area, or both, we need to go back to the drawing board and fix this, as this is the company's responsibility. In the offered example scenario, the company would want to achieve a grade of at least 90 percent, but if Susie really had not been informed of the change, or coached and supported in its use, our grades would be significantly lower, as we would have been directly responsible for the problem that arose with the client—a problem that Susie could easily have been blamed for had we not followed the process. We would have to go back and work on this to improve our grades and ensure this same problem (or other problems stemming from a similar failing on our part) didn't happen again.

THREE P'S

PROBLEM	PROCESS	PERSON
Mr. Smith's Complaints	Old Process of using consolidated statements	Susie
	New Process of Using Third Party Statements	
	Direct report properly coached on New Process	
	Susie Coached on New Process	

CLARITY	COACHING	CONDUCT
Reasonable Understanding and Clarity of Role	Need to Get feedback From Direct Report	
Have Expectations Listed Out	Has Been Attending Companies Coaching	
	Need More EG Training	
Grade 85%	Grade 80%	

One final scenario: If our "Clarity" and "Coaching" scores are 90 percent or higher, having discovered that Susie was fully trained and supported on the new changes to the system (and within her larger role), then we can finally cross the line to talk to Susie. Why? Because at this point, we can be confident that only other factor contributing to the problem is the "Person" themself—their "Conduct." At this point, we would assess *Susie's* conduct score and areas where she would need to improve in order to remain a healthy part of the business. We could walk Susie through the "Three Cs" chart and explain that she is responsible for her conduct and behaviour. At that point, Susie would have to decide whether or not she wanted to adjust her conduct and improve, her continued employment reliant in her decision, either by her own choice or ours.

By using this simple and repeatable approach instead of the classic blame game, naming the culprit and jumping to the wrong conclusions, we can be confident that we have a consistent way of fully understanding and dealing with any problem that crops up, and ensure that we are doing all we can to streamline our own processes so that recurrences are uncommon.

THREE P'S

PROBLEM	PROCESS	PERSON
Mr. Smith's Complaints	Old Process of using consolidated statements New Process of Using Third Party Statements Direct report properly coached on New Process Susie Coached on New Process	Susie

CLARITY	COACHING	CONDUCT
Reasonable Understanding and Clarity of Role Have Expectations Listed Out Grade 85%	Need to Get feedback From Direct Report Has Been Attending Companies Coaching Need More EG Training Grade 80%	If Company Grade <90% More Clarity And/Or Coaching Needed If Company Grade >90% Deal With Susie And Her Conduct

Third COO Attribute: *RELATIONSHIP WITH TIME*

*"You don't let go of a bad relationship because you
stop caring about them. You let go because you
finally start caring about yourself."*
– **Charles J Orlando**

The COO's role has the greatest connectivity to the people within the business. With these relationships comes a responsibility to ensure we respect everyone's time. We need to understand that time is the one commodity of which we only have a finite amount. This is true personally and within business as well. Too often, we think or assume that because the business is not a breathing, living entity it does not have a relationship with time. There is an old proverb that states: Time is the soul of business. We need to consider time in all aspects of our roles within the business, especially as COO. Time comes into play in a COO's role in many ways. Here are just a few:

1. Pace: This relates to the pace in which we execute the demands of our business to move at a quicker and quicker pace, in order to keep up with the vision that has been laid out. We need to respect time enough to be decisive and execute accordingly.

2. Clarity in relation to the people within the business: Too often in this area we take our time concluding whether or not a person fits within the organization. Instinctively, most people know the answer far before they actually invest their time in making changes. This hesitation is often rooted in the fact that we hold out hope for the people who do not fit. Hope that they will change, that they will learn, or that they will come to their senses. The problem for the business and

the COO is that hope is not a strategy. The larger problem with this type of thinking is that it is wasting the time of the person for whom we are holding out hope. Given what the likelihood of the outcome, an acceptance that they do not belong in your business, this is unfair to that person, whose clock is ticking away bigger and bigger chunks of their finite stores of time.

What is required is a straightforward conversation with all parties involved to decide where everyone is at. When we avoid addressing people and having tough conversations, we are not living our role as COO within the company. Instead of avoiding this type of situation, we should be embracing them. Do onto others as you would have them do unto you. If you know where you are going (and in this case where they are going), getting there sooner rather than later is the truly best thing for both parties, and much fairer on everyone than drawing things out for no purpose. Get comfortable with these types of conversations and have them in a timely fashion. To do otherwise is to do a disservice to the very people whose feelings you are wanting to spare.

3. Offering guidance to our CEO and team members: We sometimes hesitate to challenge the CEO on their thoughts on the direction of the company. We especially hesitate to give more direct feedback on their EQ and how it impacts the business. But part of your role is to hold up a mirror for the CEO to help them become the best version of themselves. And we need to do the same for everyone in the organization so they can see themselves clearly in terms of making changes that help the business. Instead, we often

waste time on behaviours, processes, and inconsistencies that rob the company of valuable time. Hold up a mirror to the whole team and all its members.

4. Outdated systems: We often continue to use systems that are not at the forefront of advancement. This slower adaptation and integration is where time comes into play. We often go slow in order to bring along the slowest people, allowing their adaptation rate to dictate the arrival time of any new system or process. The business needs to keep modernizing and using the fastest technologies, systems, and processes to propel it forward, even at the expense of some of team members' willingness to adopt it. There is a quote, generally attributed to Charles Darwin but written by Leon C. Meggison: "It is not the most intellectual of the species that survives; it is not the strongest that survives; but the species that survives is the one that is able best to adapt and adjust to the changing environment in which it finds itself." Keep changing to survive.

5. Communication: We need to improve on how the entire organization communicates with one another and ensure that the organization understands not doing so can impact time. The COO can cast a shadow that the organization follows in terms of consistency, clarity, candour, and expectations with respect to communication. The burn rate of time within a business, because of poor communication, is staggering. Most problems within a business stem from poor communication, so if we could sharpen this area, we would better respect the business's time.

6. Drift: We lose sight of the reason we were talking or having a meeting in the first place. Whether in meetings or our roles, we tend to drift away from where we should be. By having more concise meetings, we can shorten their length and waste less time. By staying in our own lanes and better executing our roles, we can become more efficient at what we do and allow others to do the same. When we "cover" someone else's work, we are just lessening the clarity of who is doing what in the business and who needs help. The COO can focus on these areas of drift to refocus a business and ensure that it is firing on all cylinders.

When we start to really think about time and how it is respected (or not) within a company, it can be a game changer. The COO has within their grasp the ability to redefine a business in this respect. Incremental changes will have a huge long-term impact. It is time to get at it.

CONCLUSION

Regardless of the size of your business, it's important to shift our mindset and start to think in the terms of the C-suite, ensuring that we can visualize both the CEO and COO roles. A business's understanding of (and adherence to) the "Vision meets Execution" approach can make a world of difference to the positivity of its outcome. On the flip side, if the "Vision meets Execution" concept is not understood (or is given a back seat in terms of priority and application), it will have a devastating impact on the business. Without the "Vision meets Execution" approach, the business will be marginalized in terms of the heights it could have reached, from either an efficiency or success point of view. This book was designed to draw your attention to these two key roles and offer my thoughts and some advice to help you understand this approach. But simply understanding it is not enough. You need to *do* something with this knowledge, and I hope this book will act as a guide, helping you to implement the mindset needed to successfully incorporate the "Vision meets Execution" approach within your business.

In both the CEO and COO role, leadership skills are on display and need to continually improve in order to bring the best version of ourselves to the business. We need to allow ourselves the understanding that this improvement is an evolution, not something that happens overnight. Within ourselves, each of us have the leadership qualities to guide our businesses to greater success.

It is time for you to step up and become the leader you should be—the leader you know you can be. Be the CEO or COO that your business deserves to have.

It will make all the difference.